Antisemitism and the left

MANCHESTER
1824

Manchester University Press

Antisemitism and the left

On the return of the Jewish question

ROBERT FINE AND PHILIP SPENCER

Manchester University Press

Published by Manchester University Press
Altrincham Street, Manchester M1 7JA
www.manchesteruniversitypress.co.uk

British Library Cataloguing-in-Publication Data
A catalogue record for this book is available from the British Library

Library of Congress Cataloging-in-Publication Data applied for

ISBN   978 1 5261 0495 3   hardback
ISBN   978 1 5261 0497 7   paperback
ISBN   978 1 5261 0496 0   open access

First published 2017

Typeset
by Toppan Best-set Premedia Limited
Printed in Great Britain
by CPI Group (UK) Ltd, Corydon CR0 4YY

To the pure, everything is pure
(in Hebrew 'la tehorim kol tahor').

(Ephraim Moses Lilien, *Ex Libris* in E.M. Lilien, *Sein Werk, mit einer
Einleitung von Stefan Zweig*, Berlin and Leipzig: Schuster & Löffler, 1903).

Ephraim Moshe Lilien, Ex Libris (Wikimedia Commons)

Contents

Acknowledgments

We have been helped, criticised and inspired by a number of people in the course of writing this book. Among those to whom we should especially like to express our gratitude (sorry for the omissions from this list) are: Christine Achinger, Claudine Attias-Donfut, Glynis Cousin, Shoshana Fine, Lars Fischer, David Hirsh, Gunther Jikeli, Alan Johnson, Lesley Klaff, Karmela Liebkind, Brendon McGeever, Sean Matgamna, Lydia Morris, Istvan Pogany, Lars Rensmann, Dave Rich, David Seymour, Karin Stoegner, Kim Robin Stoller and Howard Wollman. Institutions are vital to research and we should especially like to thank friends and colleagues in the European Sociological Association Network on Racism and Antisemitism. The discussions we have had every year since some of us succeeded in establishing the network ten years ago have been consistently stimulating, sometimes fraught and always educative. We should also like to mention the roles played by Engage – the antiracist campaign against antisemitism; Fathom – for a deeper understanding of Israel and the region; the Pears Institute for the Study of Antisemitism, Birkbeck College University of London; the Wiener Library for the Study of the Holocaust and Genocide; the Community Security Trust – protecting our Jewish community; the British Association for Jewish Studies; the Helen Bamber Centre for the Study of Rights, Conflict and Mass Violence, Kingston University; the Department of Sociology and Social Theory Centre, University of Warwick; Manchester University Press; and our enthusiastic and friendly editor Caroline Wintersgill. As always, we owe a considerable debt to our families for their engagement as well as support – to Jane, Rosa and Reuben, and to Shoshana, Tony, Glyn and Lydia. And lastly we cannot let this go without thanking the hospitable staff at Ishtar, Crawford Street, who provided us with a nourishing lunchtime 'office' where many of the ideas in this book were cooked, skewered and hashed out.

Introduction: universalism and the Jewish question

Prejudices, like odorous bodies, have a double existence both solid and subtle – solid as the pyramids, subtle as the twentieth echo of an echo, or as the memory of hyacinths which once scented the darkness. (George Eliot, *Middlemarch*)[1]

Two faces of universalism

Universalism is an equivocal principle. It shows two faces to the world: an emancipatory face that looks to the inclusion of the other on the assumption that the other is a human being like ourselves, but also a repressive face that sees in the other a failure to pass some fundamental test of what is required for membership of humanity. Supporters and opponents of universalism both capture something real and important about the phenomenon itself. Supporters remind us of universalism's emancipatory content – that it has proven to be a vital principle of civil, political and social inclusion. Opponents focus on universalism's dark side – that it has been used as a means of stigmatising, excluding and at times eliminating the 'other'. Universalism thus appears to be a complicated 'ism'. The idea that it is always 'work in progress' toward an unreachable goal is tempting but treats it as an abstract ideal that loses touch with its own social origins; the idea that it is always exclusive and exclusionary threatens to abandon any idea of universal human solidarity.

In its emancipatory aspect, the principle of universalism entails a family of ends: to treat all human beings as human beings regardless of their particular differences; to translate the abstract conception of humanity into practical legal, political and social consequences; to challenge the legitimacy of all forms of exclusion; to understand the particular differences we construct and with which we may identify – such as class, ethnicity, gender, sexuality, nationality, religion, etc. – as relative to an inherently diverse humanity; and not least to acknowledge the singularity of every individual human being. Universalism implies recognition that it is true of all human beings that our common humanity, our particularities and our unique forms of singularity enable us to shape who and what we are.

In its repressive aspect the principle of universalism serves to represent whole categories of people as inhuman, or not fully human, or not yet human, or even, in the language of Roman Law, as 'enemies of the human species' (*hostis generis humani*).[2] Many different categories of people have been turned into 'others' in analogous ways, including the enslaved, the colonised, the exploited, the orientalised, and those labelled deviant. Power and knowledge are, in this sense, deeply and mutually imbricated.

Jewish experiences of universalism have been correspondingly equivocal. Universalism has acted as a stimulus for Jewish emancipation, that is, for civil, political and social inclusion; it has also been a source (though by no means the only source) of anti-Jewish prejudice up to and beyond the classic antisemitism of the modern period. While the experience of Jews is by no means unique in this respect, one of the peculiarities of the 'anti-Judaic' tradition has been to represent Jews in some important regard as the 'other' of the universal: as the personification either of a particularism opposed to the universal, or of a false universalism concealing Jewish self-interest. The former contrasts the particularism of the Jews to the universality of bourgeois civil society; the latter contrasts the bad universalism of the 'rootless cosmopolitan Jew' to the good universalism of whatever universal is advanced – be it the nation, the race or the class. It is this negative face of universalism that has shaped what was once commonly called 'the Jewish question'. The struggle between Jewish emancipation and the Jewish question has been a struggle waged over the spirit of universalism itself and is the topic of this book.

The idea of 'the Jewish question' is the classic term for the representation of Jews as harmful to humanity as a whole. The fundamental questions it asks are about the nature of the harm Jews supposedly inflict on humanity, the reasons why the Jews are so harmful, and what is to be done to remedy this harm. The 'answers' it finds to these 'questions' are diverse within a certain semiotic unity. Among the harms Jews have been supposed to inflict are economic harms like usury and financial manipulation; political harms like betrayal and conspiracy; social harms like exclusivity and indifference toward others; moral harms like greed and cunning; and cultural harms like abstract intellectualism and contempt for nature. Among the reasons given for the harmfulness of Jews, we find reference to the restrictive conditions in which they were once forced to live, the 'tribal' assumptions of Judaism as a religion, the 'self-promotion' of Jews as the 'chosen people', the 'virulent' character of 'Jewishness' itself, and as Jean-Paul Sartre observed, the self-fulfilling effects of antisemitic labelling. Among the 'solutions to the Jewish question' that have been proffered, we find seemingly benevolent solutions such as improving the social and political conditions in which Jews live, improving the 'defective' moral character of the

Jews themselves, and combating the mindset of antisemites, as well as manifestly malign solutions like rolling back the rights of Jews, expelling Jews from their host countries to some foreign territory, and eradicating the Jews from the face of the earth.

The Jewish question signifies an asymmetric relation of others to Jews. It is an expression of the distorted face of universalism, a question that never really was a question in the first place, a question whose answers are the pre-given conditions of the question itself. And yet we find that the Jewish question keeps re-appearing in different shapes, at different times, in different places. It is like a ghost that haunts how others see Jews and sometimes how Jews see themselves. It interpellates social relations between Jews and non-Jews, Judaism and Christianity, Judaism and Islam, the Jewish nation and other nations, Jewish ideas and other ideas, etc. as if they were conflicts of a metaphysical kind between the abstract forces of inclusive universalism on one side and those of exclusive particularism on the other.

The Jewish question is premised on tearing apart the universal, particular and singular aspects of the human condition and setting them in opposition to one another. Jewish experience of the modern world has been thus punctuated by the prejudices of those who present Jewish particularity as incompatible with human universality – an opposition that may be illustrated by the Enlightenment credo that the Jew can only become a human being when he or she ceases to be a Jew, or by the antisemitic credo that the Jew *qua* Jew can never become a proper human being, or by the prejudices of those who contrast Jewish particularity with individual singularity, a contrast illustrated by the notion that *this* Jew is an *exceptional* Jew, not like the others, not like 'the Jews' as collective category, or by the antisemitic notion that the singularity of every Jew is overridden by their Jewish provenance.

The modernity of antisemitism

The term 'antisemitism' was not used until the late nineteenth century but hostility to Judaism and Jews is much older. It goes back to Greek and Persian antiquity when Judaism forbade the idol worship practised in pagan religions, but it was with the coming of Christianity that powerful anti-Judaic myths were constructed and entered deep into the structures of Western thought. Its persistence across the centuries was largely assured by the influence of religions that issued from Judaism, Christianity and Islam, which in spite of their many ethical debts to Judaism affirmed their superiority by prioritising anti-Judaism. Anti-Judaism metamorphosed over time and was partly secularised in the modern period in the domains of biology, culture and politics. In the 1870s the term 'antisemitism' was coined as an expression of resentment toward Jews by a German journalist, Wilhelm Marr, who maintained that Germans and Jews were locked in a conflict, that Jews were winning as a result of Jewish emancipation and that this conflict could only be resolved by the forced removal of Jews from Germany. Antisemitism subsequently became a crucial element of Nazi ideology and helped justify the Nazi genocide of Jews. After the military defeat of Nazism, and termination of the Holocaust, antisemitism did not simply vanish from the political landscape of Europe or majority-Muslim societies and today there are strong signs of antisemitism expressing itself afresh. Anti-Judaic ideas certainly go back to a distant past but there is also a sense in which the Jewish question is a creature of the modern age.[3]

To speak of the *modernity* of the Jewish question is to suggest first that it is not a natural or eternal 'question', second that it is reproduced and reconfigured by the conditions of modern life even at times we least expect it, and third that it is open to contestation and rarely goes uncontested. In what may broadly be termed 'the modern age', the Jewish question has been as repeatedly challenged as it has been advanced: in eighteenth-century debates on Jewish emancipation, in nineteenth-century debates on the pathologies of capitalism and aims of socialism, in twentieth-century debates on antisemitism and the 'final solution', and in twenty-first-century debates on Zionism and memory of the Holocaust. The recurrence of the Jewish question is evidence of the enduring power of inversion in the modern world. When Walter Benjamin famously pronounced that 'there is no document of civilization which is not at the same time a document of barbarism',[4] the force of this inversion was perhaps nowhere more tested than in the two faces universalism revealed to Jews. The Jewish question has multiple affinities to other modern prejudices and forms of domination that involve processes of de-humanisation, of disallowing the humanity of the other in the name of humanity, but it is the specificity of the Jewish question that concerns us here.

Left antisemitism

Antisemitism has again become an issue in our time. In recent years we have observed its re-emergence in a number of distinct political sites, including left antisemitism, Islamist antisemitism, Christian antisemitism, nationalist antisemitism and liberal antisemitism. Our focus in this book is on the contested origins of left antisemitism.

Historically, there has been no shortage either of antisemitism or of opposition to antisemitism within the left tradition. For example, the revolutionary anarchist Mikhail Bakunin wrote approvingly that 'in all countries the people detest the Jews ... so much that every popular revolution is accompanied by a massacre of Jews'. He maintained that this was a 'natural consequence' of the fact that 'this whole Jewish world ... constitutes a single exploitative sect, a sort of bloodsucker people, a collective parasite, voracious, organised in itself, not only across the frontiers of states but even across all the differences of political opinion'. He went on to claim that 'this world is presently, at least in great part, at the disposal of Marx on the one hand and the Rothschilds on the other'.[5] Bakunin was right only in one respect, that Marx was his antagonist. Marx's close collaborator Friedrich Engels also pointed to oppositions within the left when he criticised his fellow socialist, Eugen Dühring, for his anti-Judaic prejudice: 'That same philosopher of reality who has a sovereign contempt for all prejudices and superstitions is himself so deeply imbued with personal crotchets that he calls the popular prejudice against the Jews, inherited from the bigotry of the Middle Ages, a "natural judgment" based on "natural grounds", and he rises to the pyramidal heights of the assertion that "socialism is the only power which can oppose population conditions with a strong Jewish admixture" '.[6]

These two instances indicate how split the modern left tradition has been over the Jewish question: it has played a role both in representing 'the Jews' as the enemy of humanity and in combating the prejudices of those who see Jews through this lens. We should be wary of any generalisation to the effect that either 'the left is fundamentally antisemitic' or that there is no such thing as 'left antisemitism'. It remains important for us to recognise that Marx, Engels and many of those they inspired contributed far more than is usually recognised to supporting Jewish emancipation and resisting the terms of the Jewish question. In spite of the dusty clouds of interpretation that surround his work, Marx's actual writings reinforce our conviction that while there is a long tradition of left antisemitism, there is also on the left a strong *critique* of antisemitism and of the barbarism it represents. Marx's famous essays 'On the Jewish Question' were in substance a critique of the very idea of the Jewish question.

We, the authors of this book, both come from a Marxist-socialist background, whose legacy has shaped our understanding of and responses to the various distorted forms of modernity that have preoccupied us: racism, antisemitism, genocide, crimes against humanity, apartheid, ethnic nationalism, totalitarianism, etc. We recognise of course that much has gone wrong, dramatically wrong, in the name of 'Marxism' and 'the left', so much so that these names have reached the threshold of total devaluation, and that the question of antisemitism is not the least of these problems. We take it as axiomatic that those who locate themselves within this tradition *ought*, as a matter of basic principle, to combat antisemitism whenever it raises its face, but we know this is not always the case. We ought to pay attention to the experiences of those who suffer or are exposed to antisemitism and we ought not treat the self-justifications of those they challenge as a sufficient guide as to the truth of the matter. We ought to acknowledge that not all antisemites wear their conviction on their sleeve, that sometimes people may not be aware of their own antisemitic temptations, and that antisemitism can be political and cultural as well as personal. We ought to do the work of learning what antisemitism is and what shapes and forms it takes.

In these respects our relation to antisemitism ought to be no different from our relation to other forms of racism: both should be open to the liberating power of education, research, engagement, criticism and self-reflection. It should not be controversial to say that the critique of antisemitism should now be part of any emancipatory movement that seeks to *understand* what has gone wrong in the development of modern capitalist society rather than simply *blame* it on secret conspiracies or particular scapegoats.

None of this should be controversial but it has become so. We hear on the left a different refrain: notably, that antisemitism no longer matters compared with other racisms; that antisemitism was once a problem in the past but is no longer in the present; that antisemitism was a European malady that had no presence in the Islamic world; that antisemitism is understandable today given the ways Zionists behave; that the charge of antisemitism is mainly put forward for dishonest and self-seeking reasons; that people cry 'antisemitism' in order to deflect criticism of Israel; that the stigmatising of individuals and groups as antisemitic is more damaging than antisemitism itself; that the Jewish state and its supporters are the main source of racism in the modern world. It is said, for instance, that those who 'cry antisemitism' do so in order to shut down debate on Israel. This may be true in particular cases but the reverse is more plausible: that there are many who cry 'Israel' in order to shut down debate on antisemitism. When the critique of antisemitism is viewed as a problem, the problem may lie with the viewer.

Political actors with very different political agendas can and do coalesce around such rhetorics to construct a discourse with its own semblance of internal unity, its own self-justifications, its own stereotypes of external enemies and its own defence mechanisms. As this book goes to press, the British Labour Party has been struggling to come to terms with the fact that one of its leading figures, Ken Livingstone, a former mayor of London, long-term ally of its elected leader and a standard bearer of the party's left-wing, thinks that Hitler was sympathetic with Zionism before he 'went mad'. One of its newly elected MPs, Naz Shah, posted a suggestion that the simple solution to the conflict between Israel and the Palestinians was for the Jews in Israel to be relocated to the United States. Both have been accused of antisemitism and suspended from the Labour Party. In the first case, Ken Livingstone is refusing to apologise, which is consistent with the fact that for decades he has promoted the view that Nazism and Zionism are umbilically linked. By contrast, Shah has publicly acknowledged the damage such statements can make and has undertaken to reflect on the prejudice that underwrote her quip about the transportation of Jews. As we write, the Labour Party is undertaking a review of how widespread antisemitism has become in its ranks and what might be done about it. There is now more extensive public debate, of which this book is part, concerning how far ignorance and tolerance of antisemitism have affected thinking and practice within the left, most of whose members rightly pride themselves on their antiracism, and what kinds of resistance they mount collectively to rectify this situation.

A note on methodology

Misrecognition of antisemitism is both underpinned and compounded by troubling methodological assumptions that have crept into the political culture of the left and into the work of radical scholars.

The first set of assumptions we draw attention to concerns what we call the 'methodological separatism' that obscures connections between antisemitism and other forms of racism.[7] The language of antisemitism is different in important respects from that of anti-Black racism or Islamophobia and it may not be helpful to reduce them all to a generic concept like 'prejudice', partly because every form of prejudice has its own distinctive characteristics and partly because the idea of 'prejudice' does not capture all that is involved in these phenomena. To say, however, that they are not the same does not mean that they are not connected or best understood in relation to one another. A sense of the connectedness of racism and antisemitism was once viewed as the common sense of the antiracist imagination. For example, Frantz Fanon famously described Blacks and Jews as 'brothers in misery' on the grounds that racism and antisemitism both reveal 'the same collapse, the same bankruptcy of man'.[8] He cited the words of his philosophy professor: 'Whenever you hear anyone abuse the Jews, pay attention, because he is talking about you', and Fanon commented that his professor was right in the sense that 'an anti-Semite is inevitably anti-Negro'.[9] W.E.B. Du Bois remarked that it had never occurred to him that 'race prejudice could be anything but colour prejudice' until his visit to the Warsaw Ghetto gave him 'a more complete understanding of the Negro problem' as a form of 'human hate ... capable of reaching all sorts of people'.[10] He commented that 'The ghetto of Warsaw helped me to emerge from a certain social provincialism into a broader conception of what the fight against race segregation, religious discrimination, and the oppression by wealth had to become if civilisation was going to triumph and broaden in the world'.[11] The disconnection of racism and antisemitism today is suggested by the alacrity with which some antiracists respond to racism and Islamophobia but not to antisemitism, or conversely by the suspicion they show to 'charges' of antisemitism that they do not show to other forms of racism. Such responses seem to us to indicate that something has gone seriously wrong with the universalism of the antiracist imagination.

A second set of assumptions we wish to draw attention to concerns what we call the 'methodological historicism' that positions antisemitism exclusively as a phenomenon of the past. A justified refusal to treat antisemitism as a natural and permanent feature of relations between Jews and non-Jews has given way to another problematic tendency: that of situating antisemitism emphatically in the past. We may look back in horror to the period of history in which genocidal antisemitism was written into the very texture of social and political life, but console ourselves with the thought that antisemitism has, since that time, been empirically marginalised and normatively discredited. It may appear that the Holocaust has served as a learning experience concerning the dangers of antisemitism, that few in mainstream society still claim adherence to antisemitic ideologies, and that some ultra-nationalist movements are reluctant to embrace antisemitism. Liberals have paid tribute to the success of the new Europe in transcending ethnic nationalism and recognising rights of difference. Radicals have affirmed that many forms of racism still prevail in Europe but insist that antisemitism is no longer one of them. The positioning of antisemitism as a creature of the past – for instance, of a now superseded age of nationalism, late modernisation or organised modernity – serves to close our eyes to new forms it may assume in the present.

A third set of assumptions concerns the development of what we call the 'methodological dualism' that restricts our view of racism and antisemitism within a bifurcated world of 'them' and 'us'. It addresses vital distinctions – between oppressor and oppressed, power and resistance, executioner and victim, enemy and friend, imperialism and anti-imperialism, etc. – but grants them a master status that overrides all other ethical considerations. It does not treat anti-imperialism as one element within a constellation of democratic principles but turns it into an absolute truth that prevails over all other democratic principles. It is the absolutising of anti-imperialism that allows some leftist intellectuals, like Judith Butler, to declare that Hamas or Hezbollah belong to the camp of anti-imperialism and should be supported regardless of other democratic deficiencies including antisemitism.[12] The temptation on the left is simply not to see racism, antisemitism or sexism in those states and movements deemed to be in the camp of anti-imperialism, perhaps for no other reason than that they are opposed to America and Israel, and at the same time to withdraw solidarity from victims of racism, antisemitism and sexism within the camp of 'anti-imperialism'. If we label this tendency the 'anti-imperialism of fools', following in the footsteps of the Second International's labeling of antisemitism as the 'socialism of fools', this is not to indicate that anti-imperialism is foolish but rather that it is a foolish form of anti-imperialism that divorces it from wider democratic concerns.[13] The problem of methodological separatism is reinforced when racism and antisemitism are situated in opposing camps: that is, when racism is condemned as the exercise of oppressive power while antisemitism is excused as a mislabelled or misguided form of resistance. Following what David Hirsh has called a 'politics of position',[14] the same Marxist writers who deny the possibility of far-left antisemitism have been tempted to situate those who do raise concerns about antisemitism only and emphatically on the side of oppressive power and Western imperialism.[15]

The final set of assumptions we need to mention here concerns the question of 'methodological nationalism' or rather the development of a cosmopolitan critique of methodological nationalism that re-instates precisely what it criticises when it singles out one form of nationalism, in this case Jewish nationalism, as the bearer of all the defects of nationalism in general. Cosmopolitans emphasise that racism and antisemitism are not only a problem for their immediate victims but also for humanity in general and correspondingly that the responsibility to combat racism and antisemitism is a universal human responsibility.[16] They seek to resist the mimetic temptation to blame, say, 'the Germans' in the way antisemites blame 'the Jews'. It may appear 'natural' that if we are attacked as Blacks, Muslims or Jews, we fight back as Blacks, Muslims or Jews, and this semblance of the natural is confirmed by the well-established leftist credo that represents the 'nationalism of the oppressed' as the natural and rational way of responding to the racism of the oppressors. The cosmopolitan consciousness is one that does not simply negate but seeks positively to supersede this reactive standpoint. What we find today, however, is the replacement of the cosmopolitan critique of methodological nationalism by a simulacrum of cosmopolitanism that projects onto one particular instance of nationalism the defects of nationalism *in toto*. Zionism becomes here the universal equivalent of the deficiencies of all nationalism. Such singling out of *Jewish* nationalism for special opprobrium threatens both to reconfigure old stereotypes about the 'tribalism' of the Jews and to erode from within the universalistic critique of methodological nationalism.

This is not of course an exhaustive list of methodological difficulties we face in studying the elements of contemporary antisemitism that concern us here, but they hopefully suffice to indicate the difficult nature of the task. They highlight the need to reconnect racism and antisemitism as twin expressions of the same human bankruptcy, to reconnect past and present in ways that recognise the emergence of new forms of antisemitism, to reconnect domination and resistance in ways that allow for a relational understanding of the complexities of power, and to reconnect nationalist responses to antisemitism with other nationalist responses to racism. The sensitising idea that guides our work is that of reconnection. All forms of modern political life are relative to one another and universalism itself should not be thought of in emphatically absolutist terms. The little suffix '–ism' can do a lot of damage when it transforms what is relative and valid into what is absolute and invalid. As Theodor Adorno phrased it, the threat posed by universalism is to 'compress the particular like a torture instrument'.[17]

Jewish assimilationism and nationalism have both been subjective responses to the contradictions of living in an antisemitic society. One makes an 'ism' of assimilating to the norms of society as the only means of neutralising an otherwise understandable antisemitism; the other makes an 'ism' of the nation as the only means of escaping an otherwise ineluctable antisemitism. Both bear witness to the immense contradiction under these conditions between recognising our unity with others and our separate existence. Cosmopolitanism offers itself as an attractive third way for Jews living in an antisemitic world, but this 'ism' contains its own pitfalls: not only that of aloofness as a cosmopolitan world citizen from one's particular existence as a Jew but also that of accommodating to a reified cosmopolitanism that is set against the alleged particularism of Jews. We owe a debt of gratitude to cosmopolitan social scientists for putting universalism back on the agenda but to those who say that the 'humanist' universalism that once homogenised populations and repressed difference has now given way to a cosmopolitan post-universalism that respects heterogeneity and plurality, we should respond that the battle for the spirit of universalism has not so readily been resolved.[18] It is as much the illusion of progress to lock the past in the past as if it contained no alternative voices, as it is to celebrate the present in the present as if we have definitively overcome our prejudices and learned the lessons of our catastrophic history.

The future

In rejecting antisemitism as an essentialist form of turning Jews into 'others', we raise the old bogey of 'the Jewish question' in order to come to grips with a categorical frame of reference that has allowed antisemitism to flourish in the first place and that restricts opposition to antisemitism within the terms of that which it opposes. In this respect the Jewish question is to antisemitism what 'raciology', as the sociologist Paul Gilroy calls it, is to racism.[19] Sometimes antisemitism returns brazenly in the form of physical attacks on Jews *qua* Jews or on Jewish institutions. More often it slips into our political culture though the notion that something must be done to deal with the harm the Jewish state, the Jewish nation or its Jewish supporters are alleged to inflict on humanity at large.[20] Such harm, we are told, needs to be identified, explained and 'solved' for the sake of the greater good.

In his comprehensive and erudite study of the tradition of *Anti-Judaism* in modern European thought, the cultural historian David Nirenberg traces the phenomenon of anti-Judaism far back in history as an almost continuous presence within European thought. His work captures very well the recurrence of the Jewish question both in traditional and modern societies, but it is less dedicated to working out what keeps it alive in the modern world and what resistance it encounters.[21] Old prejudices continue, as George Eliot put it in *Middlemarch*, to 'scent the darkness' and 'echo in the void'. The anti-Judaic tradition is part of our cultural world, even if it is fortunately not the whole story and rarely goes uncontested.

For much of our adult lives it looked to us that there has been some progress in transcending the barbaric forms of racism and antisemitism that emerged with modern society – not least in the waging of total wars between nation states, in the brutality integral to Western domination of colonised peoples, and in the mass killings perpetrated by totalitarian regimes. For our generation, the idea of progress was given some sense of reality with the end of fascism and Stalinism, the dismantling of colonial rule, the democratisation of former dictatorships, the fall of apartheid, the unification of Europe, the development of new forms of global governance, international law and human rights, and the rise of antiracist movements. The relation between the idea and reality of progress has always been distant and difficult and faith in progress has not become any easier. Signs of barbarism were acutely visible in the 1990s in the mass murder of Muslims in Bosnia and Kosovo and the simultaneous genocide in Rwanda, and more indirectly indicated by the silence, if not effective collusion, with which these catastrophes were largely met in the 'international community'. In addition, the scepticism with which many leftist groups and individuals responded to belated top-down attempts to put a check on mass murders – through humanitarian military interventions, the formulation of a Responsibility to Protect, the extension of the concepts of genocide and crimes against humanity in international criminal law, the institution of international criminal courts, etc. – left us wondering how the idea of progress could be defended or resurrected from the bottom up.

As we moved into the new millennium, we continue to see that human rights, declared universal in 1948 in the aftermath of the Holocaust, have been denied to people in large parts of the world by a bewildering array of local tyrants and fundamentalist movements, often with the collusion of global powers who themselves can perpetrate some of the most egregious violations. The commitment made in the aftermath of the Holocaust to remove the scourge of genocide continues to be repeatedly ignored. Fleeing from violence inflicted by genocidal states, or by civil wars involving state and non-state actors, or by collapsing economies and ecologies, large numbers of refugees have sought asylum in parts of the world that appear more secure. Their journeys evoke images of human suffering present in the interwar years, which we hoped never to see again. Some find new homes but many are confronted by state borders designed to keep them out and by the hostility of populist movements. Put this together with the climate of insecurity caused by global financial crashes, state austerity programmes that pathologise the poor, and growing legitimacy problems faced by international institutions, and we may be forgiven for thinking that we find ourselves confronted by a crisis of the universal values that once underpinned our hopes of progress.

The emancipatory face of universalism remains very much in evidence – not least in the efforts of many citizens to respond personally and directly to the human suffering of minorities. 'Love is stronger than hatred', as the *Charlie Hebdo* slogan put it. And yet the crisis of universalism is deepened by a radicalism that turns its back on the universal and treats it at best as a subterfuge, at worst as a weapon of mass destruction. The return of the Jewish question is one symptom of this current crisis of universal values, which, however incompletely, provided inspiration for the more progressive ethical developments of the postwar era and without which progressive ethical developments cannot be sustained.

What will follow in this book is a discussion both of the recurrence of the Jewish question within the intellectual and political thought of the left and of the resources mobilised within the left to resist this temptation. Our book is about a long-standing struggle within the radical tradition to supersede the prejudices contained within the Jewish question and to advance more enlightened ways of thinking about the universality, particularity and singularity of human beings. It has been a tougher struggle than one might expect.

In Chapter 1 we explore debates over Jewish emancipation within the eighteenth-century Enlightenment, contrasting the work of two leading protagonists of Jewish emancipation: Christian von Dohm and Moses Mendelssohn. The former justified Jewish emancipation from within the Jewish question; the latter looked for ways of countering the prejudice that Jews were in special need of regeneration. In Chapter 2 we revisit debates between supporters and opponents of Jewish emancipation within nineteenth-century revolutionary thought, in particular the emancipatory power of Karl Marx's critique of Bruno Bauer's opposition to Jewish emancipation and endorsement of *The Jewish Question*. In Chapter 3 we explore Marxist debates (1870–1945) over the growth of antisemitism. While most Marxists were opposed to antisemitism, the mainstream downplayed opposition on the assumption that it was provoked by the ongoing harmfulness of Jews after emancipation. Deep concerns over the persistence of the Jewish question were expressed by, among others, Luxemburg and Trotsky, but we focus on the more sustained critique put forward by Horkheimer and Adorno. In Chapter 4 we discuss Hannah Arendt's critique of three types of Jewish responsiveness to antisemitism – assimilationism, Zionism and cosmopolitanism – in order to re-assess diverse ways in which the Jewish question has inserted itself into Jewish political consciousness. Chapter 5 explores debates within the left over the residues of antisemitism after the Holocaust. We focus on the endeavours of a leading postwar critical theorist, Jürgen Habermas, to counter the legacy of European antisemitism, and on the misappropriation of this project by parts of the left tempted to reinstate the Jewish question under the guise of critical theory itself. In Chapter 6 we enter into current debates within the left over representations of Israel and Zionism, focusing our critique on left antizionists who threaten to reinstate the Jewish question when they identify Israel and Zionism as the enemies of universalism. Our aim is not only to identify a tradition within the left whose thinking is deformed by the Jewish question, but also to identify a rival tradition, far more hidden from history, which has a nose for prejudice, even when it is sprayed with George Eliot's 'scent of hyacinth', and understands that the Jewish question is *in nuce* a question of antisemitism.

Notes

1 George Eliot, *Middlemarch* (London: Penguin, 1965 [1874]), 473.

2 The concept of *hostis generis humani* was originally deployed in the context of Jacobin revolutionary terror. See Dan Edelstein, *The Terror of Natural Right: Republicanism, the Cult of Nature and the French Revolution* (Chicago: Chicago University Press, 2010).

3 See Claudine Attias Donfut and Robert Fine, 'Antisemitism' in *The Encyclopedia of Social Theory*, ed. Bryan S. Turner (editor in chief), Chang Kyung-Sup, Cynthia Epstein, Peter Kivisto, William Outhwaite and J. Michael Ryan (co-editors) (Oxford: Wiley Blackwell, forthcoming).

4 Walter Benjamin, 'Theses on the Philosophy of History', Thesis VII in *Illuminations*, ed. Hannah Arendt, trans. Harry Zohn (London: Fontana, 1973), 258.

5 Quoted in Hal Draper, *Karl Marx's Theory of Revolution, Volume IV Critique of Other Socialisms* (New York: Monthly Review Press, 1990), 293–296.

6 Friedrich Engels, *Anti-Dühring* (London: Lawrence and Wishart, 1943), 126, 161.

7 See Glynis Cousin and Robert Fine, 'Brothers in Misery: Re-Connecting Sociologies of Racism and Anti-Semitism' in Efraim Sicher (ed.), *Race, Colour, Identity: Rethinking Discourses about 'Jews' in the Twentyn-First Century* (Oxford: Berghahn, 2013), 308–324.

8 Frantz Fanon, *The Wretched of the Earth*, trans. Constance Farrington (Harmondsworth: Penguin, 1967), 86.

9 Frantz Fanon 'The Fact of Blackness' in Frantz Fanon, *Black Skin, White Masks* (New York: Grove Press, 1967), www.nathanielturner.com/factofblackness.htm (8 of 23) (accessed 8 March 2008).

10 W.E.B. Du Bois, 'The Negro and the Warsaw Ghetto' [May 1952] in Phil Zuckerman (ed.) *Social Theory of W.E.B. Du Bois* (Thousand Oaks, CA: Pine Forge Press, 2004), 45.

11 Du Bois, 'The Negro and the Warsaw Ghetto', 46.

12 Judith Butler is quoted as saying: 'understanding Hamas, Hezbollah, as social movements that are progressive, that are on the left, that are part of the global left, is extremely important. This does not stop us from being critical of certain dimensions of both movements … of raising whether there are other options besides violence'. In *Judith Butler on Hamas, Hezbollah and the Israel Lobby* in teach-in, UC Berkeley, 2006 radicalarchives.org.

13 Moishe Postone, 'History and Helplessness: Mass Mobilization and Contemporary Forms of Anticapitalism', *Public Culture*, 18 (1), 2006: 93–110. We shall discus the conceptualisation of antisemitism as the 'socialism of fools' in our chapter on Marxism and critical theory.

14 David Hirsh, 'The Corbyn Left: The Politics of Position and the Politics of Reason', *Fathom*, Autumn 2015, http://fathomjournal.org/the-corbyn-left-the-politics-of-position-and-the-politics-of-reason/ (accessed 9 July 2016).

15 Alain Badiou and Eric Hazan, *L'Antisémitisme Partout: Aujourd'hui en France* (Paris: La Fabrique, 2011).

16 Hannah Arendt, *Eichmann in Jerusalem: A Report on the Banality of Evil* (Harmondsworth: Penguin, 1967), 269.

17 Theodor W. Adorno, *Negative Dialectics*, trans. E.B. Ashton (New York: Continuum, 1981), 345.

18 See Ulrich Beck and Ciaran Cronin, *Cosmopolitan Vision* (Cambridge: Polity, 2006), 30; Jeffrey Alexander, *The Civil Sphere* (New York: Oxford University Press, 2006), 465–468; Natan Sznaider, *Jewish Memory and the Cosmopolitan Order* (Cambridge: Polity, 2011), 133–147.

19 For discussion of the idea of raciology see Paul Gilroy, *Between Camps: Nations, Cultures and the Allure of Race* (London: Allen Lane, 2000), and *Against Race: Imagining Political Culture Beyond the Color Line* (Cambridge, MA: Belknap Press, 2002).

20 For critical discussion of relations between left antizionism and antisemitism in the UK, see, for example, Alan Johnson. 'The Left and the Jews: Time for a Rethink', *Fathom*, Autumn 2015, http://fathomjournal.org/the-left-and-the-jews-time-for-a-rethink/ (accessed 9 July 2016).

21 David Nirenberg, *Anti-Judaism: The Western Tradition* (New York: W.W. Norton and Co, 2014).

1

Struggles within Enlightenment: Jewish emancipation and the Jewish question

The principle of modern states has enormous strength and depth because it allows the principle of subjectivity to attain fulfilment in the self-sufficient extreme of personal particularity while at the same time bringing it back to substantial unity and so preserving this unity in the principle of subjectivity itself. The essence of the modern state is that the universal should be linked with the complete freedom of particularity and the well being of individuals. (Hegel, *Elements of the Philosophy of Right*)[1]

... you have rated me
About my moneys and my usances:
Still have I borne it with a patient shrug,
For sufferance is the badge of all our tribe.
You call me misbeliever, cut-throat dog,
And spit upon my Jewish gabardine,
And all for use of that which is mine own.
Well then you now appear to need my help
(Shylock, Shakespeare: *Merchant of Venice*)[2]

Equivocations of Enlightenment

The intellectual and political revolutions of the eighteenth century provided the springboard for the 'long century of Jewish emancipation' that followed.[3] They triggered the lifting of legal barriers that restricted where Jews could live, what professions they could enter and what schools they could attend. In turn, the upshot of these legal reforms included the geographical mobility of Jews from villages and small towns to the major cities of Western and Eastern Europe – Warsaw, Vienna, Berlin, Budapest, London, Paris – and the social mobility of Jews from small traders and middlemen to the professions, business, arts and sciences. Bit by bit, one step forward and one back, with all manner of local and national variations, the universalism intellectually articulated in the eighteenth-century Enlightenment, and politically actualised in the American and French Revolutions, set in motion processes that allowed the Jews of Europe to enter the modern world. Enlightenment universalism thus prepared the way for the abolition of the old order in which Jews were designated a separate 'nation' within their various host societies, permitted to have their own religious and legal institutions, and yet subjected to all manner of occupational, fiscal, residential and political discriminations. The subordinate status of Jews had left most Jews in poverty, vulnerable to external persecution from the Church, state and people, and dependent internally on their own rabbinical and financial elites. The Enlightenment project was to bring this old order to an end and integrate Jews into society as autonomous human beings of a certain faith or indeed of no faith at all.[4]

This was the emancipatory face of Enlightenment universalism. Its repressive face was to prepare the grounds for the long gestation of modern antisemitism that occurred in the nineteenth century. Universalism was wielded as a stick with which to beat Jews by the simple device of representing Jews as the enemy of universalism. In the Enlightenment, these two faces of universalism, that of Jewish emancipation and that of the so-called 'Jewish question', were bound tightly together.

In a perceptive essay on *Enlightenment and the Jewish Question* (1932), Hannah Arendt caught very well the ambiguities of Enlightenment universalism as far as relations to Jews were concerned. She observed that even 'our great *friend* Dohm' – she was referring to Christian von Dohm whom she described as the 'outstanding advocate' of Jewish emancipation in Prussia – put forward an idea of emancipation that was 'the source of a great deal of mischief'.[5] To illustrate what kind of 'mischief' Arendt had in mind, she quoted a passage from Dohm's 1781 text on *The Civic Improvement of Jews*:

> It would be better if the Jews, along with their prejudices, did not exist – but since they do exist, do we really still have a choice from among the following: to wipe them off the face of the earth; ... or to let them remain in perpetuity the same unwholesome members of society they have been thus far; or to make them better citizens of the world.[6]

Dohm opted not to wipe the Jews 'off the face of the earth' or to leave them the 'same unwholesome members of society' but for the third option: to 'make them better citizens of the world'. The 'mischief' Arendt identified was that 'from the start the Jew became *the* Jew' – an abstraction removed from the lives of actual Jews. The superficially innocent use of the definite article in statements about 'the Jews' turned out to be not so innocent at all.[7] The use of the phrase 'the Jews', as in 'the Jews killed Christ', has a quite different connotation from a sentence without the definite article, as in 'Jews were involved in killing Christ', which no longer attributes to the category of 'the Jews' guilt for this action even if it recognises that some Jews were involved. In the use of the definite article what is at issue is the *abstraction* of 'the Jews' as a homogeneous collectivity or a collectivity with an essential nature even if individual Jews could be treated as 'exceptions'. Arendt read Dohm's text as the product of a liberal, reforming consciousness prepared to wager that 'even the Jew is a human being – the most improbable thing of all', and prepared to treat the emancipation of Jews as a 'test case for human rights' in the sense of testing whether *even the Jews* could be improved by a regime of equal citizenship. Arendt maintained that this way of thinking about Jewish emancipation was common in the Enlightenment and destined to turn 'advantage into disadvantage when economic assimilation ... turned an oppressed and persecuted people into bankers, merchants and academics'. She wrote:

> Friends became foes once they were forced to observe that living Jews were not universally oppressed ... the heirs of the Enlightenment, who had insisted on emancipating the Jews along with the rest of humanity, ... now accused the Jews of turning emancipation into a privilege they demanded for themselves and not for all oppressed peoples ... former friends finally became antisemites themselves.[8]

We might add that when 'the Jews' were later presented within the antisemitic imagination as still more harmful after emancipation than they had been before, this was taken as proof that the corruption of Jews was not the result of the oppressive conditions to which Jews were subjected but of the unchanging nature of the Jews themselves. Arendt observed that the idea of a 'solution to the Jewish question', which the Enlightenment deployed in support of political emancipation, was to become the conceptual ground on which modern antisemitism was built. As she put it, 'The classic form in which the Jewish question was posed in the Enlightenment provides classic antisemitism its theoretical basis'.[9] Even in Dohm, the champion of Jewish emancipation, the assumption was that there was a 'Jewish question' and that Jewish emancipation could only be justified in terms of 'solving' it.

If we consider more closely Dohm's essay *Concerning the Amelioration of the Civil Status of the Jews* (*Über die Bürgerliche Verbesserung der Juden*), we find a powerful argument for the political emancipation of Jews posed in terms of solving the Jewish question.[10] As Dohm saw it, the role of government was to 'mitigate the mutually exclusive principles' of the various groups, religions and classes that constitute society, 'so that all the single notes are dissolved in the great harmony of the state'. He maintained that the basis of good government was for members of different social groups, religions and classes to 'consider their separateness as secondary and their role as citizen primary'. Following this line of argument, Dohm wrote that 'if actually in the faith of today's Jews there should be some principles which would restrict them too strongly to their special group and exclude them from the other groups of the great civil society', the answer was not to persecute them further, which would 'only serve to confirm them in their opinions', but to improve their status.

Dohm acknowledged the force of the old accusations laid against the corruption of the Jews: they entertained 'such bitter hatred of all who do not belong to their tribe' that they were unable to look at them 'as members of a common civil society with equal rights'; they manifested such 'lack of fairness and honesty in ... commerce' and acted in ways so 'harmful to the welfare of the rest of the citizens' as to render it 'justified to issue restrictive laws against this nation'; they showed 'exaggerated love ... for every kind of profit, usury and crooked practice' as well as 'antipathy against other religions'. Dohm did not deny the corruption of the Jews, only the conclusions drawn from it. His response was to point out the error in the reasoning of those opposed to Jewish emancipation: 'one states as cause what in reality is the effect'. Dohm explained Jewish corruption in terms of 'the hard and oppressive conditions under which the Jews live almost everywhere' and held that it was 'very natural that these conditions cause the spirit of the Jew to lose the habit of noble feelings ... to debase him in his activities ... to choke every sense of honour in his heart'. He argued that 'everything the Jews are blamed for is caused by the political conditions under which they now live' and that 'any group of men, under such conditions, would be guilty of identical errors'. He put it in material terms: 'every kind of occupation and trade has some special effects on the way of thinking and the moral character' of those who practice it. Concerning Jews who 'had been forced for many centuries now to live on commerce exclusively', he concluded:

> Is it surprising that the spirit of this occupation became entirely their spirit ... ? Love of profit must be much more vivid in the Jews because it is the sole means of survival for them ... If this reasoning is correct, then we have found in the oppression and in the restricted occupation of the Jews the true source of their corruption. Then we have discovered also at the same time the means of healing this corruption and of making the Jews better men and useful citizens.

Dohm's Enlightenment credo was that improvement in the civil status of Jews would improve the Jews:

> The Jew is even more a man than a Jew, and how would it be possible for him not to love a state where he could freely acquire property and freely enjoy it, where his taxes would be not heavier than those of other citizens, where he could reach positions of honour and enjoy general esteem? ... The Jew will not be prevented by his religion from being a good citizen, if only the government will give him a citizen's rights.[11]

Dohm concluded that it was up to 'us', presumably Christians, 'to induce the Jew to feel humanly by proving that we have such feelings ourselves. In order to heal him of his prejudices against us, we first have to get rid of our own'.

Dohm was by no means alone in justifying Jewish emancipation in terms of solving the Jewish question. In the French Enlightenment, for example, Abbé Gregoire (1750–1831), who actively supported abolition of slavery as well as Jewish emancipation, still justified the latter in terms of enabling the 'moral and physical regeneration of Jews'.[12] There were Jews who shared this perspective. Isaac Berr (1744–1828), one of a group of six Jews from Alsace Lorraine who came to the Assembly in Paris to defend Jewish emancipation, wrote to fellow Jews in 1791 that it was the start of a process in which 'we' (in this case Jews) must 'work a change in our manners, in our habits, in short, in our whole education ... and divest ourselves entirely of that narrow spirit of Corporation and Congregation in all civil and political matters'.[13] In 1789 Comte Stanislas de Clermont-Tonnerre, arguably the outstanding supporter of Jewish emancipation in France, stood up for the civil and political rights of Jews before the National Assembly on the grounds that emancipation would serve to remedy the corruption of Jews – visible economically in the practice of usury, and politically in the practice of acting as a 'nation within the nation':

> Usury ... so justly censured is the effect of our own laws. Men who have nothing but money can only work with money: that is the evil. Let them have land and a country and they will loan no longer: that is the remedy ...

> The Jews have their own judges and laws ... that is your fault and you should not allow it. We must refuse everything to the Jews as a nation and accord everything to Jews as individuals ... It is repugnant to have in the state an association of non-citizens and a nation within the nation'.[14]

Clermont-Tonnerre did not say that Jewish emancipation should be dependent on Jews abandoning their Judaism in favour of the single identity of French *citoyen*, but that the subordinate status of Jews as a 'nation within the nation' had to be superseded in the name of egalitarian universality and that the idea of treating Jews as a 'nation' at all had to be rejected as 'repugnant'. This idea was to become a hostage to fortune when the 'repugnant' idea of forming a Jewish nation was turned into a movement and an actuality.

Arendt was certainly right that formulation of the Jewish question in Enlightenment thought acted as a conceptual foundation for the antisemitism to come, but wrong to insist on the unanimity of the Enlightenment and downplay its plurality and capacity for social learning. Within the consciousness of Enlightenment figures with a reputation for lack of sympathy to Jews, we find surprising ambivalences. Sometimes they were expressed through the mouths of fictional characters to convey an empathetic representation of Jews and Judaism standing up for universal principles of justice in contrast with a cruel and broken Christianity. In 1761 Voltaire, whose comment that 'biblical Jews' were the 'most detestable people on the earth' is regularly quoted by historians of antisemitism, authored a powerful protest against the Inquisition, delivered through the mouth of a fictional Rabbi of Smyrna. The 'Rabbi' called for universal recognition of 'all the children of Adam, whites, reds, blacks, greys' as fellow human beings and condemned an *auto-da-fé* in Portugal in which, Voltaire wrote, a Jesuit, two monks, two Muslims and thirty-two Jews were burned to death. Concerning the condemned Jews Voltaire's Rabbi had this to say:

> What was their crime? Nothing other than that of being born [Jews] ... Can you believe that while the flames devoured these innocent victims, the Inquisitors and the other savages chanted our own prayers? The Grand Inquisitor himself intoned the *makib* of our good King David, which began with these words: 'Have pity on me, O my God, according to your great mercy' ... Thus these pitiless monsters invoked the God of mercy and kindness, the forgiving God, while committing the most atrocious and barbarous crimes ... by a contradiction as absurd as their fury is abominable, they offer to God our *makibs*, they borrow our religion itself, while punishing us for having been brought up in our own religion.[15]

Like a ventriloquist who puts his better self into the voice of his dummy, Voltaire intoned, through his Rabbi, a powerful protest against the double standards of the Christian Church and its projection onto Jews of the cruelty that it itself demonstrated.

We find similar ambivalences in Montesquieu. He is quoted by historians of antisemitism for a comment in *Persian Letters* that 'You can be sure that wherever there is money, there are Jews' and for another in *The Spirit of the Laws* that 'commerce passed to a nation covered with infamy and was soon distinguished only by the most frightful usury, monopolies, subsidies, and all dishonest means of acquiring money'. He also adopted, however, the guise of an anonymous Jew to remonstrate against the burning of a ten-year-old Jewish girl in an *auto-da-fé* in Lisbon:

> You put us to death, who believe only what you believe, because we do not believe *all* that you believe. We follow a religion, which you yourselves know to have been formerly dear to God. We think that God loves it still, and you think that he loves it no more: and because you judge thus, you make those suffer by sword and fire, who hold an error so pardonable as to believe that God still loves what he once loved. If you are cruel to us, you are much more so to our children; you cause them to be burnt because they follow the inspirations given them ...
>
> You would have us be Christians, and you will not be so yourselves. But if you will not be Christians, be at least men: treat us as you would, if having only the weak light of justice which nature bestows, you had not a religion to conduct ... If you have this truth, hide it not from us ... The characteristic of truth is its

triumph over hearts and minds, and not that impotency which you would confess when you would force us to receive it by your tortures ... if any one in times to come shall dare to assert that in the age in which we live the people of Europe were civilized, you will be cited to prove that they were barbarians; and the idea they will have of you, will be such as will dishonour your age and spread hatred over all your contemporaries.[16]

Through the mouth of this fictional Jew, Montesquieu attacked the false universalism of Christians whose own claim to humanity was premised on projecting inhumanity onto the Jews. These passages from Voltaire and Montesquieu raise the question of what the torture and murder of Jews in the name of Christianity says about Christians themselves. They indicate the presence of an internal struggle within Enlightenment thought: it was both immersed in the muddy waters of the Jewish question and it opened up the space for emancipatory ways of thinking that were fiercely critical of the status quo.

The great cosmopolitan philosopher of the eighteenth century, Immanuel Kant, undoubtedly reflected the wider prejudice against Jews to be found in the Enlightenment when he opined that for Jews 'all estimation of other men, who are not Jews, is totally lost, and goodwill is reduced merely to love of their own tribe', and cast doubt on the prospect of converting this nation of 'Palestinian swindlers' into productive citizens.[17] Kant's contraposition of universalism to the Jews was in line with other equally stereotypical comments on non-European peoples in his *Anthropology*. However, Kant had some 'second thoughts' in the wake of the French and Haitian Revolutions concerning the terrible injustices non-Europeans suffered at the hands of European colonialism: second thoughts, we may speculate, provoked in part by learning about the actual revolts waged against the existing state of injustice (like that of the Black Jacobins in San Domingue), in part by engaging in dialogue with those who actually belonged to the groups suffering from prejudice (as Kant did with the Jewish Enlightenment figure, Moses Mendelssohn), and in part by embarking on new intellectual voyages (like his studies in the last decade of his life into the cosmopolitan development of the system of right in what became his *Metaphysics of Justice*). He did not express similar second thoughts about Jews, but he developed close relations with individual Jewish scholars and took a relatively liberal position on Jewish emancipation.[18]

Kant's legacy was split between those who accentuated his anti-Judaism and those who applied his cosmopolitanism to Jews. Among those who emphasised the Jewish question, David Michaelis cited as obstacles to Jewish emancipation a religion that kept Jews from 'intermingling' with others and that cast serious doubts on their political loyalty. Johann Gottlieb Fichte opposed Jewish emancipation on the grounds that the Jews acted as a 'state grounded in the hatred of the entire human race ... a powerful hostile state that lives with all others in constant warfare ... spreading through almost all the lands of Europe and terribly oppressing its citizens'. Fichte was an enthusiast for the universalism of the

French Revolution but his vista of universalism was paired with a vision of winning the war against the Jews – whether through the guillotine or by some other means.[19]

The emancipatory face of Kant's cosmopolitanism signified that all exclusions, of which the exclusion of Jews was one, had to be justified according to the normative expectation of equal freedom of all human beings. Kant gave expression to a powerful logic of inclusion that enabled struggles for recognition to be waged by the excluded classes themselves and their allies.[20] Unsurprisingly, perhaps, the Enlightenment voices that were most critical of the Jewish question were also Jewish voices.[21] The Jewish philosopher, Moses Mendelssohn (1729– 1786), a pivotal figure in the dissemination of Kant's philosophy, made a deep and passionate case for severing the links between Jewish emancipation and the Jewish question far more radically than Kant had been able to do. He had solicited Dohm's essay *Concerning the Amelioration of the Civil Status of the Jews* and had registered his approval of a work that meant that 'the Rights of Man are beginning to be taken to heart'. He also wrote, however, that he looked forward, for 'that happy time when attention will be given to human rights in all their proper compass'. His concern was that Enlightenment had 'not trodden down all the tracks of barbarism in history', including barbarism toward Jews, and that 'prejudice' was continuing to put 'obstacles in the way of our civil admission'.[22] Mendelssohn rejected the notion that Jews needed 'improvement' or that there was anything in the observance of Jewish law that was not compatible with the imperatives of philosophical universalism – except, that is, the coercive force the old order had wrongly endowed Jewish councils with as the property of Jewish juridical autonomy. Once this system was overcome and unrestricted freedom of religion introduced, Jewish difference was no obstacle to the unity and diversity of humankind. Mendelssohn maintained that all special restrictions on Jews and all special privileges of Jews must be ended, whether or not they enabled amelioration in the behaviour of Jews, and repudiated Dohm's contention that the Jews were not yet fit for the full citizenship implied by a bar on their entry into the high ranks of the civil service and military. If 'civil union' required abandoning the Jewish way of life, Mendelssohn argued, 'we must rather do without civil union'.[23] Dohm had not made support for Jewish emancipation *conditional* on the improvement of Jews but he did present emancipation as the *sine qua non* of 'improvement'. Mendelssohn called on Jews to remain 'stiff-necked' in the face of any pact that demanded abandonment of 'harmful' Jewish laws and customs in return for emancipation, and drew parallels between the prejudices of those who once sought to transform Jews into Christians and those who now sought to transform Jews into 'useful citizens'. He not only defended the social utility of usury, an offence with which Jews were so often charged, but he also put forward as a universal principle the credo that no one should be considered 'useless' – not the 'pauper', not the 'cripple' and not the Jew.[24] Mendelssohn's stress on the universality of Jewish Law appeared to Kant as a backward, heteronomous step compared with his own stress on the moral autonomy of all rational human beings, but it was Mendelssohn who revealed the very real danger embodied in the idea of Christian supersession: that 'the Jews' were being turned into the personification of all that was going wrong in Europe at the time.[25]

The meaning of Enlightenment and the equivocations of the revolutionary tradition

What do the equivocations shown by Voltaire, Montesquieu, Dohm and Kant, the anti-Judaic prejudices shown by Michaelis and Fichte, and the critiques developed by Mendelssohn and Ascher signify for our understanding of Enlightenment's relation to Jewish emancipation and the Jewish question? It is one of Enlightenment debate rather than unanimity. We should be wary of an overly critical reading of Enlightenment universalism we find arising from some sources. For example, in a chapter of *Anti-Judaism* entitled 'Enlightenment Revolts Against Judaism' David Nirenberg puts his emphasis on the common anti-Judaic typifications that kept recurring among the *philosophes*: abuse of money, disposition to cruelty, intolerance toward other peoples, unthinking obedience to the law, obstinate defence of particularism, resistance to the universality of the Christian world-religion, etc.[26] The intellectual historian of antisemitism, Arthur Hertzberg, concludes his study of *The French Enlightenment and the Jews* on a similar note with the judgment that 'modern, secular anti-Semitism was fashioned not as a reaction to the Enlightenment and the Revolution, but within the Enlightenment and Revolution themselves'.[27] The American sociologist, Jeffrey Alexander, comments on the 'failure of universalism' indicated by the 'endemic inferiority' projected onto the Jews by Enlightenment *philosophes*.[28] The French sociologist, Shmuel Trigano, comments that the Enlightenment *philosophes* treated Jews as 'hostages of the universal'.[29] The British sociologist, Victor Seidler, declares that within the terms of Enlightenment universalism Jews were expected to give up their Jewishness as part of the price of emancipation: 'if they were to remain as Jews it would be in the private sphere alone'.[30] Arendt, as we have seen, focused in her early essays on Enlightenment's affinity to the Jewish question at the expense of its emancipatory potential. The inclination of these judgments has been to draw strong conclusions about the pitfalls of Enlightenment universalism. They are partially justified but do not capture the whole. Enlightenment was certainly neither fixed nor homogenous in its attitudes.

In practice, the Enlightenment logic of universality could be declarative rather than actual, but it represented a huge step forward for a European tradition, which had, since the Treaty of Tordesillas of 1494, taken for granted the duality between public law inside Europe and colonial domination outside Europe, and which had, since the Alhambra Decree of 1492 expelling Jews from the Iberian Peninsular, taken for granted the duality between public law for 'Europeans' and exceptional status for those deemed to be 'oriental'. The same universal principles of equality that appeared in the 1789 Declaration of the Rights of Man and Citizen were then invoked by the Black Jacobins of San Domingue, who fought for their own emancipation from slavery with the Marseillaise on their lips, joined forces with French revolutionaries in the *Society of the Friends of Blacks* including Mirabeau and Talleyrand, and lobbied successfully for the abolition of slavery to be included in the 1793 Declaration of the Rights of Man and Citizen.[31] The same universal principles were invoked by Jews, be it under different circumstances, who protested against the refusal of revolutionary deputies in France to grant them equal rights in December 1789 because of their alleged ethical failings, and who lobbied more successfully for the right to Jewish emancipation in 1791. The development of universalism was not only a 'Western' phenomenon, far from it, but in the West it set in motion legal and political demands that went far beyond its own original terms. The universal constitutional principles developed in eighteenth-century revolutions were marginalised, betrayed, distorted and reversed but nonetheless survived as resources of resistance. They signified that the rights of man and citizen belonged to everyone, that the violation of the rights of one particular group of people should be treated as a violation of the universal rights of all, and that those who spoke in support of rights spoke for the whole society and not only for one group within it.

It is an observed paradox of emancipation that prejudice is never far behind. Alexis de Tocqueville argued that a paradoxical relation existed between slave emancipation and social discrimination in the United States. He observed that racial prejudices were stronger in the north where slaves were emancipated than in states where slavery still persisted, and that as black people became citizens in northern states they were also prevented from participating in civic life. The more legal arrangements erased distance between black and white, the more whites recreated distance for fear of blending with those they saw as 'inferiors'. It was in the emancipated north, he argued, that skin colour became the criterion on which social distancing was based, whereas in the south (where social status was legally defined in terms of a master–slave relation) proximity was tolerated under the control of the masters.[32] In the case of Jews, we have seen that emancipation was in part a legal process by which states removed civil and political disabilities restricting Jewish minorities, and afforded Jews equal civil and political rights. It was also meant to be a social process that demanded that Jews should no longer be regarded as intrinsically alien but be accepted as an integral part of society. It was theoretically possible for these two processes, legal and social, to come together and reinforce one another. The countervailing tendency, however, was to breed a mood of resentment within French society that focused on the injustice of treating 'inferiors' as equals, the dangers of treating 'aliens' as citizens, and the harm that came of rendering Jews less distinct and less visible.

Ressentiment was expressed from different ends of the political spectrum based on the notion that the 'improvement' of Jews should have been made the pre-condition of emancipation or that the harmfulness of Jews was proving unchangeable.[33] Arendt characterised the problem of social recognition thus: 'society, confronted with political, economic and legal equality for Jews, made it quite clear that none of its classes was prepared to grant them social equality, and that only exceptions from the Jewish people would be received'.[34]

The equivocations of Enlightenment thought were mirrored in revolutionary practices, whose failure to find solutions to the social, national and democratic questions they faced, opened up a space within the revolutionary tradition itself for the Jewish question to show an increasingly ugly face. Arendt's much mis-understood analysis of the French revolution can in this context be revealing. She argued that a solution to the *social question* was urgent since no revolution was possible where the masses were weighed down by poverty. The Jacobins made herculean efforts to solve this problem but the political means they employed proved 'futile' and 'dangerous'.[35] In their 'compassionate zeal for the poor' they sought to transform *les malheureux* into *les enragés* by blaming their misfortune on those they saw as having betrayed the trust of the people – venal military leaders, corrupt political leaders, foreign agents, unprincipled speculators – whom they designated 'enemies of the people' or 'enemies of humanity'.[36] Arendt argued that a solution to the *democratic question* was equally urgent in a society previously subjected to monarchical absolutism. Again, the Jacobins made efforts to solve this problem but their conception of revolutionary democracy was reduced to a uniform and homogenised image of 'the people' as a 'multi-headed monster … always in the right', in which the value of individuals was judged by the extent to which they subsumed their individuality to the 'will of the people'.[37] This way of thinking about revolutionary democracy subordinated the vibrant public life the revolution had once generated to a world of increasingly universal suspicion in which responsibility for setbacks was attributed to those accused of putting their private interests before the interests of 'the people'. Finally, Arendt argued that a solution to the *national question* was needed. The Declaration of the Rights of Man and Citizen affirmed the inalienable dignity of every individual human being no power on earth could deny, but it derived all rights from the nation and blended its conception of universal rights with the duty of uncondi-tional obedience to the nation that granted these rights. At the dawn of the Revolution, decrees were passed granting French citizenship to resident foreign-ers; foreign societies and newspapers were encouraged; support was offered to foreign revolutionaries; and foreign 'benefactors of humankind' (including Tom Paine, William Wilberforce and Mary Wollstonecraft) were awarded honorary citizenship. This spirit of hospitality was not to last.[38] The fate of Tom Paine, the man who signed himself 'humanus', is indicative: he was impoverished, impris-oned and finally expelled.[39] The rights of citizens and foreigners became a matter of indifference compared with the survival of the state.

Our argument is that the failure of revolutionaries to find answers to these pressing social, democratic and national questions paved the way for their replacement by the singular 'question' of who was to be held culpable of betraying the revolution. The answer to this question was not necessarily 'the Jews', but the question itself rendered the revolutionary tradition vulnerable to the conspiracy thinking that became the hallmark of the Jewish question.[40] It would be wrong to conclude that the modern revolutionary tradition reinforced the 'failures of universalism' already evident in the Enlightenment, but this does not mean that the seeds of a reconfigured Jewish question were not present within it.

Notes

1 Hegel, *Elements of the Philosophy of Right*, ed. Allen Wood (Cambridge: Cambridge University Press, 1991 [1820]), 124.

2 Shylock, Shakespeare: *Merchant of Venice*, Act 1, Scene 3, lines 106–114.

3 In 1791 the French National Assembly annulled all legal barriers to citizenship 'affecting individuals of the Jewish persuasion'. It meant that Jews, in principle, could secure civic integration without the quid pro quo of conversion to Christianity or the provision of special, financial services to the state. See Pierre Birnbaum and Ira Katznelson, *Paths of Emancipation* (Princeton: Princeton University Press, 1995), 3.

4 Key dates in the uneven process of Jewish emancipation were that of British Jews 1866; Jews of the Austro-Hungarian Empire 1867; Italian Jews 1870; German Jews 1871; Swiss Jews 1874; Russian Jews 1917; and Polish, Romanian and Baltic Jews 1919. This list of dates does not reveal, however, the dance of death played between the granting and withdrawal of rights to Jews.

5 Hannah Arendt, 'Enlightenment and the Jewish Question' in Hannah Arendt, *The Jewish Writings* (New York: Schocken Books, 2007 [1932]), 3–18; emphasis in original. See also Hannah Arendt, *The Origins of Totalitarianism* (New York: Harcourt Brace, 1979 [1951]), 12.

6 This passage is quoted in 'Antisemitism' in Arendt, *The Jewish Writings*, 64, but should be treated with some caution since we have as yet been unable to locate this passage in Dohm's writings.

7 See the insightful discussion of the term 'the Jews' in Berel Lang, 'On the "The" in "The Jews": From Grammar to Anti-Semitism', *World Zionist Organization*, 9 October 2015, www.wzo.org.il/index.php?dir=site&page=articles&op=item&cs=3130&lang page=eng (accessed 9 October 2015).

8 Arendt, 'Antisemitism', 63.

9 Arendt, 'Antisemitism', 64.

10 Christian von Dohm, *Concerning the Amelioration of the Civil Status of the Jews* (1957 [1781]), http://germanhistorydocs.ghi-dc.org/pdf/eng/15_TheJews_Doc.3_English. pdf (accessed 15 July 2015). There are no page numbers in the electronic edition.

11 For discussion of the Jewish Question in Germany see Paul Lawrence Rose, *Revolutionary Antisemitism in Germany* (Princeton: Princeton University Press, 1992) and

Enzo Traverso, *The Jews and Germany*, trans. Daniel Weissbort (Lincoln: University of Nebraska Press, 1995).

12 According to Grégoire, Jews were to be cleansed of their particularity and 'melted into the national mass'. Abbé Grégoire, *An Essay on the Physical, Moral and Political Reformation of the Jews* [1789], extract in Paul Mendes-Flohr and Jehuda Reinharz (eds.), *The Jew in the Modern World: A Documentary History* (Oxford: Oxford University Press, 1995), 49–53. See Ronald Schechter, *Obstinate Hebrews: Representations of Jews in France 1715–1815* (Berkeley: University of California Press, 2003), 'Introduction'.

13 Cited in Jay Berkovitz, *The Shaping of Jewish Identity in Nineteenth-Century France* (Detroit, Michigan: Wayne State University Press, 1990), 73.

14 Cited in Lynn Hunt, *Inventing Human Rights: A History* (London: W.W. Norton and Company, 2008), 155–158.

15 This quotation is drawn from Voltaire's 'The Sermon of Rabbi Akib' and cited by Paul Berman in 'Jews, Muslims, Liberals, PEN Boycotters Beware: Voltaire is Laughing at You: Is the Enlightenment Philosopher Having a Moment?' *Tablet*, 1 May 2015, http://tabletmag.com/jewish-arts-and-culture/books/190669/pen-boycotters-voltaire (accessed 2 May 2015). Voltaire's text is available in G.K. Noyer (ed.), *Voltaire's Revolution: Writings from His Campaign to Free Laws from Religion* (Amherst: Prometheus Books, 2015).

16 Montesquieu, *The Spirit of the Laws*, XXV, 13 (Berkeley: University of California Press, 1977), 351–352.

17 Kant, *Anthropology From a Pragmatic Point of View*, ed. and trans. Robert B. Louden; introduction by Manfred Kuehn (Cambridge: Cambridge University Press, 2006), 100.

18 Pauline Kleingeld, 'Kant's Second Thoughts on Race', *The Philosophical Quarterly*, 57 (229), October 2007: 573–592; Robert Bernasconi, 'Kant's Third Thoughts on Race' in Stuart Elden and Eduardo Mendieta (eds.), *Reading Kant's Geography* (Albany: State University of New York Press, 2011), 291–318.

19 Fichte wrote: 'I would see no other way to give the Jews civil rights than to cut off their heads in one night and put others on them in which there would not be a single Jewish idea'. Gottlieb Fichte, *Contribution to the Correction of the Judgments of the Public on the French Revolution* [first published 1793], quoted in Jonathan Hess, *Germans, Jews and the Claims of Modernity* (New Haven: Yale University Press, 2002), 140.

20 On the universalism of the Enlightenment and revolutionary tradition see Hauke Brunkhorst, *Critical Theory of Legal Revolutions: Evolutionary Perspectives* (London: Bloomsbury, 2014), 9–57; Robert Fine, 'Enlightenment Cosmopolitanism: Western or Universal?' in David Adams and Galin Tihanov (eds.), *Enlightenment Cosmopolitanism* (London: Legenda, 2011), 153–170; and Sankar Muthu, *Enlightenment Against Empire* (Princeton: Princeton University Press, 2003). It was a disgrace that the non-European world was treated as a sphere of occupation, expropriation and expansion and excluded from the protection of the European law of nations. Imperialism presupposed the difference between the rule of law in the home country and 'the merry dance of death and trade' in colonised territories, immortalised in Joseph

Conrad's *Heart of Darkness*. The reverse side of *Ius Publicum Europaeum* was the transformation of the rest of the world into the property of European sovereigns and corporations. As Arendt observed, 'the agents of the force of expansion felt no obligation to man-made laws. The only law they obeyed was the law of expansion' (Arendt, *Origins*, 215). The practices of imperialist-minded businessman 'whom the stars annoyed because he could not annex them' were to be internalised in the European world (Arendt, *Origins*, 144).

21 In a universalistic vein, the socialist Leon Blum inverted antisemitic imagery when he wrote in the 1930s, that 'the Jews' religion is justice'. See Pierre Birnbaum, *Léon Blum: Prime Minister, Socialist, Zionist* (New Haven: Yale University Press, 2015).

22 See Shmuel Feiner, *Moses Mendelssohn: Sage of Modernity* (New Haven: Yale University Press, 2010), 139–144. Feiner quotes from Moses Mendelssohn's 'Preface' to his German translation of Ben Israel's *Vindiciae Judaeorum* [1782].

23 See Shmuel Feiner, *Moses Mendelssohn*, 178. Feiner quotes from Moses Mendelssohn, *Jerusalem: Or on Religious Power and Judaism* (Boston: Brandeis 1983). To Dohm's contention that aspects of the old order of Jewish legal autonomy should be maintained, including powers of excommunication held by rabbinical leaders, Mendelssohn demanded immediate removal of all rabbinical powers to enforce religious discipline. Jewish reformation was not to be imposed under duress but it was to be an autonomous process of self-emancipation.

24 Feiner, *Moses Mendelssohn*, 143. See also Jonathan M. Hess, *Germans, Jews and the Claims of Modernity* (New Haven: Yale University Press, 2002), ch. 3 'Mendelssohn's Jesus: The Frustrations of Jewish Resistance', 91–136.

25 The Jewish reformist, Saul Ascher, similarly maintained that the emergent political anti-Judaism of his time, delivered from the lectern rather than the pulpit and from the perspective of secular rather than Christian universalism, shared the same premise, the need for Jewish improvement, but was still more sinister than that which preceded it. Who would have thought, he wrote in relation to Fichte's anti-Judaic polemics in his *Contribution to the Correction of the Judgment of the Public on the French Revolution*, that 'decapitation would have found followers in Germany who want an entire nation to be improved by such an experiment'. He saw that for Fichte 'the Jew' is the first bone of contention in every society – the hydra that destroys everything in its path' (147). Ascher inverted the old Christian hierarchy, by presenting Judaism and not Christianity as the basis of a genuinely universal religion, and along with Mendelssohn challenged the denigration of Judaism central to the Kantian image of modernity and idea of progress. See Hess, *Germans, Jews and Modernity*, ch. 4 'Philosophy, Antisemitism and the Politics of Religious Reform: Saul Ascher's Challenge to Kant and Fichte', 137–168.

26 David Nirenberg, *Anti-Judaism: The History of a Way of Thinking* (London: Head of Zeus, 2013).

27 Arthur Hertzberg, *The French Enlightenment and the Jews: The Origins of Modern Antisemitism* (New York: Columbia University Press, 1990), 7.

28 Alexander, *The Civil Sphere*, 459–548.

29 Shmuel Trigano, *La République et les Juifs après Copernic* (Paris: Presse D'aujourd'hui, 1981).

30 Victor Seidler, *Shadows of the Shoah: Jewish Identity and Belonging* (Oxford: Berg, 2000).

31 See C.L.R. James, *The Black Jacobins: Toussaint L'Ouverture and the San Domingo Revolution* (New York: Vintage, 1989 [1938]); and Susan Buck-Morss, 'Hegel and Haiti', *Critical Inquiry*, 26 (4), 2000: 821–865.

32 Alexis de Tocqueville, *Democracy in America*, ed. and trans. Harvey Mansfield and Delba Winthrop (Chicago: University of Chicago Press, 2000). In his sociological study of the caste system in India, Louis Dumont also traces how legal distinctions between masters and slaves were replaced by racial distinctions recreating hierarchy in egalitarian societies. Louis Dumont, 'Caste, racisme et stratification' in *Homo Hierarchicus: Le Systeme des Castes et ses Implications* (Paris: Gallimard, 1966).

33 The term 'antisemitism', coined by a journalist Wilhelm Marr in 1871, became the banner under which opposition to Jewish emancipation was given ideological expression. See Marr, *The Victory of Judaism over Teutonism* (1879). See Rose, *Revolutionary Antisemitism in Germany*.

34 Arendt, *Origins*, 56.

35 Hannah Arendt, *On Revolution* (Harmondsworth: Penguin, 1990 [1963]), 222; 114.

36 See Edelstein, *The Terror of Natural Right*, 4; 86.

37 Arendt, *Revolution*, 94. Arendt's account of the dialectics of revolution had much in common with that of Hegel, who repeatedly returned to the philosophical significance of the French Revolution in his philosophical writings, including *Early Theological Writings* (Philadelphia: University of Pennsylvania Press, 1975), *Phenomenology of Spirit* (Oxford: Oxford University Press, 1977 [1807]), *Elements of the Philosophy of Right*, and *Philosophy of History* (London: Dover, 1956). See Robert Fine, *Political Investigations: Hegel, Marx, Arendt* (London: Routledge, 2001), 61–78.

38 See Florence Gauthier, 'Universal Rights and National Interest in the French Revolution' in Otto Dann and John Dinwiddy (eds.), *Nationalism in the Age of the French Revolution* (London: Hambledon, 1987). The turn against foreigners, inaugurated in the Terror, was a significant aspect of the rolling back of democracy, which continued into the Napoleonic period. See Isser Woloch, 'The Contraction and Expansion of Democratic Space during the Period of the Terror' in Keith Baker (ed.), *The French Revolution and the Creation of Modern Political Culture*, vol. 4 (Oxford: Pergamon, 1994).

39 See Julie Kristeva, *Strangers to Ourselves* (New York: Columbia University Press, 1991), 154–167.

40 Jews generally benefitted from the Revolution, but faced discrimination and some persecution during the Terror and then under Napoleon. In 1808 Napoleon's *décret infâme* reduced, postponed or annulled all debts with Jews and restricted where Jews could live. Ten years later these restrictions were abolished. See Bernard Harrison, *The Resurgence of Antisemitism: Jews, Israel and Liberal Opinion* (Lanham, Maryland: Rowman and Littlefield, 2006), 163–172; Ronald Schechter, *Obstinate Hebrews*, ch. 5 and ch. 6; Simon Schwarzfuchs, *Napoleon, The Jews and the Sanhedrin* (London: Routledge and Kegan Paul, 1979); Patrick Girard, *La Révolution Française et les Juifs* (Paris: Robert Laffont, 1989).

2

Marx's defence of Jewish emancipation and critique of the Jewish question

The Jew ... must cease to be a Jew if he will not allow himself to be hindered by his law from fulfilling his duties to the State and his fellow-citizens. (Bruno Bauer, *Die Judenfrage*)[1]

The Jews (like the Christians) are fully politically emancipated in various states. Both Jews and Christians are far from being humanly emancipated. Hence there must be a difference between political and human emancipation. (Marx and Engels, *The Holy Family*)[2]

Capitalism has not only doomed the social function of the Jews; it has also doomed the Jews themselves. (Abram Leon, 'Toward a Solution to the Jewish Question')[3]

Within the eighteenth-century Enlightenment, the perspectives of Jewish emancipation and the Jewish question were synthesised to the extent that emancipation was justified in terms of solving the Jewish question. Within the French Revolution, the inclusive face of universalism that was articulated in the Declaration of the Rights of Man and Citizen was synthesised with the terror directed at those labelled 'enemies of humanity'. In both the Enlightenment and the revolutionary tradition, however, there were alternative ways of thinking about Jewish emancipation that sought to break radically from the prejudicial assumptions of the Jewish question. In the nineteenth century, the synthesis of Jewish emancipation and the Jewish question was to be torn apart. On the one hand, the Jewish question was set in opposition to Jewish emancipation; on the other hand, Jewish emancipation was justified independently of the Jewish question.[4] The tensions contained in the eighteenth-century synthesis could no longer be held in check.

In the 1820s, the emergent opposition between Jewish emancipation and the Jewish question may be illustrated through the debate between the older and allegedly more conservative Hegel and the radical German populist and student radical, Jacob Fries. In a pamphlet titled *On the Danger Posed to the Welfare and*

Character of the German People by the Jews, Fries maintained that the harm caused by Jews was such that they should be prohibited from establishing their own educational institutions, marrying Gentiles, employing Christians as servants or entering Germany, that they should be forced to wear a distinctive mark on their clothing and that they should be encouraged to emigrate.[5] Fries' depiction of the Jews as the enemy of the people was coupled with the revolutionary conviction that all political *life must derive exclusively from the people, a category from which the Jews were excluded.*

Hegel argued that the superficial attraction of Fries' radical populism was the mix of 'heart, friendship and enthusiasm' on which it was based, but he maintained that the hatred and contempt Fries showed for rights, law and the state was 'the chief shibboleth whereby false friends of "the people" give themselves away'. Hegel demonstrated that it is a matter of 'infinite importance' that 'a human being counts as such because he is a human being, not because he is a Jew, Catholic, Protestant, German, Italian, etc.' and that when we speak of Jews as *human beings* 'this is not just a neutral and abstract quality ... for its consequence is that the granting of civil rights gives those who receive them a *self-awareness* as recognised *legal* persons in civil society'. Hegel repudiated those who sought to deny civil and political rights to Jews on the pretext that the Jews were a foreign nation and not an integral part of the people: 'If they had not been granted civil rights, the Jews would have remained in that isolation with which they have been reproached, and *this would rightly have brought blame and reproach upon the state which excluded them*'.[6]

Hegel's robust repudiation of Fries' false radicalism was, as it were, the first salvo of a struggle resumed twenty years later, in the 1840s, in the debate between the radical 'Young Hegelian' Bruno Bauer and Karl Marx over the Jewish question in Germany. Paradoxically, it was in the spirit of the 'conservative' Hegel that Marx distanced himself from the 'radical' Young Hegelian. It is to this debate we now turn.

Re-reading Marx

Two views prevail concerning Marx's own relation to the Jewish question. The *disparaging view* is that Marx, notwithstanding his Jewish origins, was an antisemite *avant la lettre* and that he made use of antisemitic stereotypes and tropes in his critique of capitalism. This view is pronounced among scholars of modern antisemitism and draws sustenance above all from the second of Marx's two 1843 essays 'On the Jewish Question', where he appears to link Judaism with the cult of money, and to associate human emancipation with emancipation from Judaism. His writings have been situated in a tradition Julius Carlebach calls 'the radical critique of Judaism' – a tradition that prefigured the 'left antisemitism' to come.[7]

The *apologetic* view adopted above all by Marxist commentators has tended to *ignore* the seemingly antisemitic aspects of Marx's writings, or to *trivialise* them as passing prejudices that did not enter into his scientific work, or to *normalise* them as a characteristic sign of Marx's own times, or to *translate* them into a more acceptable language of anti-capitalism (e.g., by translating *Judentum* into '*commerce*'), or, finally, to defend them on the grounds that they reflected accurately the social role of Jews at the time. We are critical of both these ways of reading Marx.

The problem with the disparaging view is that, beyond the second essay, 'On the Jewish Question', there is not much compelling evidence of anti-Judaic thinking in Marx's writings. Marx is accused of deploying racist and antisemitic epithets in private correspondence with Engels. An often-cited case is his depiction of Ferdinand Lassalle as '*Jude Itzig*', a term used by Jews to mock the grandiose pretensions of other Jews. Marx was referring in this letter to Lassalle's predilection for the pseudo-science of physiognomy. In another letter to Engels, Marx made fun of Lassalle's own 'smooth, self-important, vainglorious, deceitful charlatan's physiognomy' and in yet another he expostulated that Lassalle 'proved by his cranial formation and hair' that he 'descends from the Negroes who had joined Moses' exodus from Egypt'.[8] In reading this private correspondence, we may accuse Marx of bad taste or chuckle at his acerbic wit but there is no evidence that he had anything other than disdain for Lassalle's belief in physiognomy and for the authoritarian and illiberal conception of socialism of which this was part. Marx was clearly making fun of his socialist opponent.

There is occasional use of anti-Jewish epithets in Marx's political articles. In an article entitled 'The Russian Loan', probably written by Engels but published under Marx's name in the *New York Daily Tribune* (4 January 1856), 'Marx' writes: 'We find every tyrant backed by a Jew, as is every Pope by a Jesuit. In truth, the cravings of oppressors would be hopeless, and the practicality of war out of the question, if there were not an army of Jesuits to smother thought and a handful of Jews to ransack pockets … The real work is done by the Jews, and can only be done by them … as they monopolise the machinery of the loan-mongering mysteries'. Was Marx's attack on *Jewish* finance alongside that on *Jesuit* ideology antisemitic? Two years earlier (15 April 1854) he had expressed outrage over the poverty of Jews in Ottoman-ruled Jerusalem, commenting: 'Nothing equals the misery and the sufferings of the Jews at Jerusalem, inhabiting the most filthy quarter of the town … the constant objects of Mussulman oppression and intolerance'. *Whether* or not any of these articles should be considered antisemitic, or Islamophobic or anti-Catholic, we may leave to our readers. We might well wish to place them in a tradition of radical criticism of the 'economic Jew' – not unlike, say, Irene Nemirovsky's critique of a rich Jewish merchant modelled on her father in her 1929 novel *David Golder*.[9]

The more telling objection to this reading of Marx, however, lies in the unequivocal support he and Engels gave to Jewish emancipation in Germany and in the very strong opposition they expressed toward left thinkers who either opposed Jewish emancipation or made it conditional on Jews in some way 'improving' themselves. Many of the left intellectuals Marx and Engels most strongly criticised had antisemitic or proto-antisemitic leanings: not just the young Hegelian Bruno Bauer, to whom Marx's essays 'On the Jewish Question' were a response, but also the anarchist Pierre-Joseph Proudhon, the co-operative socialist Charles Fourier, the radical philosopher Eugen Dühring, the insurrectionist socialist Louis-Auguste Blanqui, and the revolutionary anarchist and pan-Slavist, Mikhail Bakunin.[10] Marx's and Engels' criticisms of these and like-minded authors were directed in part at their anti-Jewish prejudices and more especially at the political and intellectual limitations of which these prejudices were symptomatic. These critiques indicate how actively and purposefully Marx and Engels confronted anti-Judaic and antisemitic currents running through the 'left'.

When we turn to the apologetic view of Marx's relation to antisemitism, we find that it is no better grounded. The proposition that Marx's thinking was universalistic and, as such, incompatible with antisemitism can only be sustained if one ignores the Enlightenment legacy. The proposition that Marx's stereotyping of Jews was a valid attempt to explore the rational kernel of the Jewish question presupposes the truth-content of anti-Judaic prejudices: for example, that the Jews demand their own rights but not those of others, that the Jews stand for their own emancipation but not for the general cause of emancipation, that the Jews exempt Judaism from normal procedures of open criticism, etc. Some commentators endorse what they take to be Marx's own view, that Jewish emancipation should have been postponed until Jews superseded their Judaism or that the sooner Judaism disappeared, the better it would have been for society and for the Jews themselves. Some commentators have failed to distinguish Marx's views from Bruno Bauer's anti-Judaic contentions, for example, that 'the same people … who watch with pleasure when Christianity is subjected to criticism are capable of condemning anyone who also wants to subject Jewry/Judaism to criticism', or Bauer's equally anti-Judaic contention that 'the defenders of Jewish emancipation have hence appropriated the odd position of fighting against privileges and at the same time granting Jewry/Judaism the privilege of immutability, invulnerability and unaccountability'.[11] Some have more disgracefully defended Marx's second essay 'On the Jewish Question' on the grounds that it revealed the real links that existed between Judaism and the 'spirit of the usurer and the trickster'.[12] The legacy of this misreading of Marx has been to encourage Marxists to work on the assumption that there was a 'Jewish question' to solve and to encourage scholars of antisemitism to treat Marx and Marxism as part of the problem.[13]

We argue that both interpretations, the disparaging antisemitic interpretation and the apologetic Marxist interpretation, conceal what is innovative and original in Marx's contribution to the *critique* of the Jewish question. In opposite ways they both serve to situate Marx within the bounds of the Jewish question. We need to find a way of re-reading Marx and his actual texts without the weight of this ideological baggage. At stake here for us is not just how to evaluate Marx himself but also how to recognise and reconstruct a tradition of critical theory that is able to face up to the phenomena of antisemitism.

The grammar of Marx's critique of the Jewish question

In a contribution to public debate on the Jewish question in Germany, Bruno Bauer, a Young Hegelian and radical theologian, put his weight behind the cause of humanity to which, he argued, Judaism was fundamentally hostile. According to Bauer, while human history is a process of development, the Jews have shown themselves incapable of evolving with it: they cannot grow spiritually as human beings; they have no care for universal human concerns; by presenting themselves as the 'chosen people' they purport to stand apart from and above all other human beings; they claim discrimination at the hands of European society but actually exercise prodigious financial power over it. If Jews are to be considered for emancipation, Bauer concluded, they would have to demonstrate commitment to the general cause of humanity and they could do so only by abolishing Judaism. As Bauer put it: 'As long as he is a Jew, the restricted nature that makes him a Jew will inevitably gain the ascendancy over the human nature which should join him as a man to other men'.[14] Bauer may be read as radicalising the restrictions on Jewish emancipation imposed by the Jewish question.

In Marx's first essay 'On the Jewish Question' he begins with his own paraphrase of Bauer's argument:

> You Jews are egoists if you demand a special emancipation for yourselves as Jews. You should work as Germans for the political emancipation of Germany and as men for human emancipation and you should look upon the particular form of oppression and shame which you experience not as an exception to the rule but rather as a confirmation of it ... The Jew by his very nature cannot be emancipated ... The Jew himself can behave only like a Jew towards the state, i.e. treat it as something foreign, for he opposes his chimerical nationality to actual nationality, his illusory law to actual law, he considers himself entitled to separate himself from humanity, he refuses in principle to take any part in the movement of history, he looks forward to a future which has nothing in common with the future of humankind as a whole, and he sees himself as a member of the Jewish people and the Jewish people as the chosen people.[15]

Marx then unravels step by step the poverty of Bauer's theory. Bauer anachronistically based his attack on Judaism on the role once played by Jewish finance in the development of capitalism but no longer operative. He pathologised this role as wholly negative and naturalised it as an essential property of Judaism.

Other critics of Bauer had revealed his ignorance of contemporary Jewish life. According to Moses Hess, for instance, Bauer's association of *Judentum* with egoism revealed that he knew little about Jewish society: 'Nothing is more foreign to the spirit of Judaism than the egoistic salvation of the isolated individual ... No nation refutes egoism more strongly than the Jewish'. Heinrich Heine declared wittily, 'Some think they know the Jews because they have seen their beards'.[16] Marx's approach was different: it was not to challenge Bauer on the empirical grounds that Jews were not as bad as he portrayed them to be, but rather to turn the argument on its head and challenge the assumptions that lay behind it. Jews were manifestly a more complex, differentiated, plural and class-divided category of people than Bauer acknowledged, but the issue was how to release the question of Jewish emancipation from the grip of the so-called Jewish question.[17]

Marx supported Jewish emancipation unequivocally and without conditions: 'We do *not* tell the Jews that they cannot be emancipated politically without radically emancipating themselves from Judaism, which is what Bauer tells them'.[18] While Bauer asked why Germans should be interested in the liberation of the Jew if the Jews were not interested in the liberation of the Germans, Marx inverted this question: 'Does the standpoint of political emancipation have the right to demand from the Jews the abolition of Judaism and from man the abolition of religion?'[19] To Bauer's assertion that 'the Christian state ... cannot allow adherents of another particular religion ... complete equality with its own social estates', Marx observed that in France (partially) and North America (more fully) Jews, like Christians, are politically emancipated and concluded that states which did not yet politically emancipate Jews must be rated negatively by comparison with the 'perfected political state' and shown to fall short.[20] Marx understood that the Jewish question was in actuality a German question: it was not about the Jews but about Germany's capacity to enter the modern world. Behind Bauer's opposition to Jewish emancipation was an inability to understand how modern society works. Freedom of religion does not mean freedom *from* religion but the right to be religious or not in any way one wishes. In the United States, Marx observed, there was no state religion and yet it was 'the land of religiosity *par excellence*'.[21] Religious freedom does not signify abolition of religious commitments and distinctions, but only of their political significance for suffrage, property rights and occupational access. Freedom of religion signifies that religion becomes a private right and the state becomes a secular state.

Marx did not reject the distinction Bauer adopted between political and human emancipation but what he did with it was contrary to what Bauer did with it. Bauer appealed to human emancipation *against* political emancipation, maintaining that to overcome the egoism, false equality and abstraction of rights was the condition of creating the 'real harmonious species-life of man'.[22] Marx treated the Declaration of the Rights of Man and Citizen as a 'great step forward',[23] which marked the difference between 'the modern representative state and the old state of privileges' and which for the first time turned the 'affairs of state into the affairs of the people'.[24] Marx recognised the limits of political emancipation: 'The fact that you can be politically emancipated without … renouncing Judaism shows that *political emancipation by itself is not human emancipation*'.[25] This recognition was not designed, however, to devalue political emancipation or treat it as a mere stepping-stone to be discarded once human emancipation was achieved, but to redeem it as a necessary though insufficient component of human emancipation. Marx perceived an *intrinsic relation* between political and human emancipation: political emancipation is not human emancipation but there can be no human emancipation without political emancipation. Marx famously observed that 'not one of the so-called rights of man goes beyond egoistic man, man as a member of civil society, namely an individual withdrawn into himself, his private interest and his private desires, and separated from the community'.[26] This comment appears to indicate congruity between Marx and Bauer to the extent that both considered right to be an expression of bourgeois egoism, but the logic of Marx's argument is quite different from that of Bauer: it is that since none of the rights of man goes beyond the egoistic individual separated from the community, it makes no sense to exclude the Jews on the grounds of their alleged egoism and separation from the community.

The language of the second essay 'On the Jewish Question' is nevertheless troubling. Let us quote from the Penguin translation to give a flavour of just how troubling:

What is the secular basis of Judaism? Practical need, self-interest. What is the secular cult of the Jew? Haggling. What is his secular God? Money. Well then! Emancipation from haggling and from money, i.e. from practical, real Judaism, would be the same as the self-emancipation of our age … We therefore recognise in Judaism the presence of … a contemporary anti-social element whose historical evolution – eagerly nurtured by the Jews in its harmful aspects – has arrived at its present peak, a peak at which it will inevitably disintegrate. The emancipation of the Jews is in the last analysis the emancipation of humankind from Judaism … Money is the jealous God of Israel before whom no other God may stand … Exchange is the true God of the Jew. His God is nothing more than illusory exchange … What is present in an abstract form in the Jewish religion – contempt for theory, for art, for history, for man as an end in himself – is the actual and conscious standpoint, the virtue, of the man of money … The chimerical nationality of the Jew is the nationality of the merchant, of the man of money in general … The ungrounded and unfounded law of the Jew is only the religious caricature of … the purely formal rites with which the world of self-interest surrounds itself. Here too the supreme relation of man is the legal relation, the relation of laws which apply to him not because they are the laws of his own will and nature but because they dominate him and because breaches of them would be avenged … As soon as society succeeds in abolishing the empirical essence of Judaism – the market and the conditions which give rise to it – the Jew will have become impossible … The social emancipation of the Jew is the emancipation of society from Judaism.[27]

This text summarises rather succinctly the key prejudices contained in the Jewish question and endorsed by Bauer. Should we read these prejudices as representative in any way of Marx's own views? If so, how are we to treat the relation between Marx's defence of Jewish emancipation and critique of the Jewish question in the first essay, written only weeks earlier, and this mouthful of anti-Judaic stereotypes in the second? One possible answer is that Marx was more like Bauer than we suggest, the difference between them boiling down to the difference between one who demands that Jews give up Judaism *as a condition of* political emancipation and one who advances political emancipation for Jews in the hope and expectation that they will then give up their Judaism. This interpretation, however, cannot explain the second essay's discontinuity with his first essay or indeed with Marx and Engels' biting restatement of their critique of Bauer in *The Holy Family* written shortly afterward. In this text, Marx and Engels were even more scathing about Bauer's attempt to justify the exclusion of Jews from political society in terms of their self-exclusion from civil society, to debase not just Jewish emancipation but political emancipation as such as the 'illusion of the masses', and label Marx and Engels themselves derogatorily as 'representatives of the mass': 'How low "the mass" is in comparison with holy criticism', Marx and Engels jibed in response.[28]

If we are to retain the unity of Marx's three responses to Bauer – that is, the first and second essays on the Jewish question and then parts of *The Holy Family* – we need to trace the common logic running through them. We can do so along the following lines.

Since the rights of man and citizen include freedom of religion, what grounds can there be for excluding Jews because of their religion?

Since the rights of man include rights of egoism, what grounds can there be for denying civil rights to Jews because of their alleged egoism?

Since the rights of citizen abstract 'political man' from their social role, what grounds can there be for excluding Jews because of their allegedly harmful social role?

Since money in modern society is the supreme world power, what grounds can there be for denouncing Jews for allegedly turning money into their God?

While Bauer represents the Jew as 'moneyman', Marx responds that in the modern world 'money has become a world power'. While Bauer imagines that money is 'the practical spirit of the Jews', Marx responds that money has also become 'the practical spirit of the Christian peoples'. While Bauer says that money is the 'jealous God of Israel', Marx responds that the God of the Jews has become the God of the world. After Marx, no longer can the defence of Jewish emancipation be grounded in assumptions about the goodness of 'Christian civil society' or the badness of 'Jewish tribalism'.

This interpretation of Marx has the advantage of upholding the unity of his texts. It also gives body to a universalism that has no truck with the Jewish question. The real question for Marx was whether a backward state like Germany could catch up with modern states like the US and France, which had already granted equal rights to Jews. His defence of Jewish emancipation drew sustenance from the radical wing of Enlightenment in its radical attack on the whole mindset of the Jewish question. It was not just a critique of Bauer but of the Jewish question itself and of the place it occupied in Enlightenment and the modern revolutionary tradition. Bauer went on to paint Jews as 'white Negroes' and to propose shipping Jews to 'the land of Canaan'; Marx and Engels went on to develop their critique of the economic forms of capitalist society. There lies a fundamental and critical difference.

Real humanism and the Jewish question

We do not wish to suggest that there was nothing in any of Marx and Engels' conception of human emancipation that was not open to being read through the lens of the Jewish question, only that this reading misconstrues the 'real humanism' they sought to nurture. As the philosopher Karl Löwith puts it in his monograph *Max Weber and Karl Marx*, Marx sometimes appeared to identify human emancipation with 'emancipation from every kind of particularity in human life as a whole; from the specialisation of occupations just as much as from religion and privatisation'.[29] In *History and Class Consciousness* the Marxist philosopher, Georg Lukács, maintained that the consciousness of the worker under capitalism becomes no more than the 'self-consciousness of the commodity' and that it is only when every particular human element has been taken away that workers can begin to conceive of human emancipation 'uncontaminated by any trace of reification'.[30] A conception of human emancipation as emancipation from every kind of particularity – property, family, gender, religion, nationality, occupation, etc. – appears to leave no space for the particularity of Judaism. If 'the Jews' are viewed through the lens of the Jewish question as the very personification of the particular, it becomes but a short step to conclude that for Marx emancipation from Judaism was a crucial step in the emancipation of humanity from all particulars and all traces of reification. It is hard to imagine in these interpretations of human emancipation what place there could be for Jews or Judaism in the communist future. This reading of human emancipation might appear to be anticipated by the homage Marx and Engels paid in *The Communist Manifesto* to the dissolving effects of bourgeois society:

> The bourgeoisie cannot exist without constantly revolutionising the instruments of production and thereby the relations of production, and with them the whole relations of society ... Constant revolutionising of production, everlasting uncertainty and agitation distinguish the bourgeois epoch from all earlier ones. All fixed, fast frozen relations, with their train of ancient and venerable prejudices and opinions, are swept away ... All that is solid melts into air ... All that is holy is profaned ... The bourgeoisie ... has left no other bond between man and man than naked self-interest ... The bourgeoisie has resolved personal worth into exchange value ... The bourgeoisie has drowned ... religious fervour ... in the icy waters of egoistical calculation ... The bourgeoisie has stripped of its halo every occupation hitherto honoured ... The bourgeoisie has torn away from the family its sentimental veil.[31]

In imagery drawn from Shakespeare's *Tempest*, capitalist society is portrayed as leaving no other nexus between human beings than that of naked self-interest. All particulars – property, culture, family, marriage, childhood, education, country, religion, morality, occupation, personal worth – are reduced to a money relation. There is nothing that bourgeois society cannot destroy and surpass – even itself.

In facing up to the revolutionary iconoclasm of the bourgeoisie, Marx and Engels express no nostalgia for the annihilated past, but endeavour to turn the destructive nihilism of the bourgeois into the affirmative communism of the proletarian. Since workers are left like Nietzsche's 'last man' without name, individuality or place, nothing can be taken from them because all has already been taken: workers become slaves to capital, appendages to the machine, commodities to be bought and sold on the market place, for whom all values appear as bourgeois prejudices. If communism is their movement and has no interests apart from those of the proletariat as a whole, then the aim must be to abolish particularity for all since capitalism has already abolished it for the masses. The workers have a world to win, not by restoring old values, but by harnessing the destructive energy of bourgeois culture for the creation of a more human world.

After the defeats of the 1848 revolutions, the crucial development in Marx's political thought lay in his recognition that the modern worker is *not* a commodity but the owner of commodities and therefore a person, a human being in the substantial sense of the term. Workers have more to lose than their chains, which is just as well if they have a world to win. While their labour-power has been turned into a commodity, they themselves have become subjects, owners of their own labour-power, possessors of at least this form of property. It is this quality of personality belonging to workers that Marx sees as the beginning of their long and arduous journey in the development of human self-emancipation.

What arose against and after Marx was a tendency within official Marxism to turn the denial of the right of particularity into a fixed doctrine: to treat human beings as units in a chain of determined circumstances, to evaporate the active side of human life and to reify the universal. One of the manifestations of this 'heresy against man', as the Marxist historian Edward Thompson aptly put it, was to make possible the reconfiguration of the Jewish question. This was not the path taken by Marx and Engels, who came to recognise that workers in capitalist society are not mere commodities but *owners* of commodities, at least their own labour-power, and that they are therefore rights-bearing subjects with more to lose than their chains. The defence of subjective rights developed by Marx after 1848 was continuous with that of the young Marx in his critique of the Jewish question. Neither Marx nor Engels were afraid of combating forms of 'socialism' that were capable, as they put it in *The Communist Manifesto*, of no more than 'hurling the traditional anathemas' against bourgeois liberties and representing the Jews as 'a secret world power which makes and unmakes governments'.[32]

For Bauer and those 'Marxists' who followed in his footsteps, human emancipation was premised on imagining 'a world without Jews', but the vista of human emancipation Marx and Engels put forward was shaped by an altogether less repressive vision. In the final paragraph of Marx's first essay he introduced the following formulation:

> Only when real individual man resumes the abstract citizen into himself and as an individual man has become a species-being in his empirical life, his individual work and his individual relationships, only when man has recognised and organized his *forces propres* as *social forces* so that social force is no long separated from him in the form of *political* force, only then will human emancipation be completed.[33]

The meaning of this passage is not self-evident but we find here a conception of human emancipation that is not based on excluding 'the Jews' for failing some test of human universality but on developing individuality to its maximum extent and overcoming the dominance of abstraction over human life. The exemplar of the dominance of abstractions over human life is that of 'the Jews' over real individual Jews. 'Real humanism' is predicated on recognising the humanity of Jews in their individuality, that is, in their empirical life, work and relationships. In defending Jewish emancipation against the restoration of the Jewish question, Marx re-affirmed the subjective right of Jews to be citizens, to be Jews, and to deal creatively, singularly, in their own way, with their Jewish origins. Real humanism is a revolt against the tyranny of provenance.

The humanist Marx we are endeavouring to uncover is doubtless not the only Marx we could find, and we are aware that we have to shake off thick clouds of interpretive obfuscation to see its outlines. Our conviction, though, is that an interpretation of this kind does justice to the unity and integrity of Marx's texts, as well as to an authorship that would have no truck with the repressive demands of the Jewish question even in its left wing manifestations. Marx's early essays on the Jewish question actually ushered in a lifelong critique of antisemitism. They showed that the point of view of the Jewish question is not an inevitability; that it can be overcome. Marx's essays remain, for all their ambiguities, a key resource for recovering a tradition of critical thought that repudiates 'left antisemitism'. We should be sceptical both of the claim that Marx personally or politically exhibited anti-Jewish prejudices and of the claim that this was in some fundamental way characteristic of the left. What seems more important to us is that Marx fought against the mainstreams of contemporary radicalism and socialism, which were drawn to the assumptions of the Jewish question and in some cases helped to reconfigure it. This is not say that Marx should bear no responsibility for becoming dramatically and fatefully misappropriated, since the ambiguities of his second essay on the Jewish question, and of his writings on human emancipation, allowed the Jewish question to be smuggled back in. The Marx we find, however, is the child of Enlightenment who struggled to emancipate the Enlightenment from its own anti-Judaic prejudices. His contribution was to dissociate the right to rights of all human beings from substantive notions of particular communal worth, to justify the right of Jews to emancipation without resort to any form of the Jewish question (including Jewish claims to the universality of Judaism), to demonstrate the ties that bound the Jewish question to a wider devaluation of human rights, and to map the poisoned terrain on which modern antisemitism was rising. He was not alone in this endeavour but his voice became ever harder to hear over time as antisemitism set in and the Jewish question also infused its opposition. It is to Marxist appropriations and misappropriations of Marx's critique of the Jewish question that we now turn.

Notes

1 Bruno Bauer, *Die Judenfrage* (*The Jewish Question*).
2 Karl Marx and Friedrich Engels, *The Holy Family or Critique of Critical Criticism: Against Bruno Bauer and Company* (Moscow: Progress, 1980).
3 Abram Leon, 'Toward a Solution to the Jewish Question', *The Jewish Question: A Marxist Interpretation* (New York: Pathfinder Press, 1979 [original French edition, 1946])
4 For a more general discussion of how the Enlightenment synthesis broke into extremes, see Karl Löwith, *From Hegel to Nietzsche* (New York: Anchor, 1967), 240ff.

5 See Shlomo Avineri, *Hegel's Theory of the Modern State* (Cambridge: Cambridge University Press, 1972), 119–121. He characterises the political current represented by Fries as 'proto-fascist'.

6 Hegel, *Elements of the Philosophy of Right*, 'Preface', 15–16. Emphasis in original.

7 Among compelling examples of the disparaging view of Marx's proto-antisemitism are: Julius Carlebach, *Karl Marx and the Radical Critique of Judaism* (London: Routledge and Kegan Paul, 1978); Francis Kaplan, *Marx Antisémite?* (Paris: Berg International, 1990); Edmund Silberner, 'Was Marx an Antisemite?', *Historica Judaica*, 2 (1), 1949: 3–52; Rose, *Revolutionary Antisemitism in Germany*, 296–305; Paul Johnson, *A History of the Jews* (London: Phoenix, 1994), 350–352; Shlomo Avineri, 'Marx and Jewish Emancipation', *Journal of the History of Ideas*, 25 (3), 1964: 445–450; Alexander, *The Civil Sphere*, 485–488; and Nirenberg, *Anti-Judaism*, 430–439.

8 The quotations are drawn from letters from Marx to Engels on 6 June 1853, 30 July 1862, and 29 May 1863. See Karl Marx and Friedrich Engels, *Letters*, www.marxists.org/archive/marx/letters/date/ (accessed 28 November 2015).

9 Julius Carlebach records that at the time of Marx's 1843 writings small traders and hawkers constituted 66% of the Jewish working population in Prussia and the great majority of the working population in Eastern Europe. Marx acknowledged the historic role of some Jews in commerce and moneylending in pre-modern societies but saw it replaced by more systematic processes of national capital accumulation. See Carlebach, *Karl Marx*, 56.

10 For firm evidence of their antisemitism see Pierre-André Taguieff, *La Judéophobie des Modernes: des Lumières au Jihad Mondial* (Paris: O. Jacob, 2008).

11 The misappropriation of Marx by Marxists on the Jewish question is discussed in depth in Lars Fischer's *The Socialist Response to Antisemitism in Imperial Germany* (Cambridge, New York: Cambridge University Press, 2007), 37–102. The passages Fischer quotes here (pp. 53–54) are from Franz Mehring, one of the leading Marxist intellectuals of the Second International. Elsewhere Mehring writes: 'Marx regards Judaism as a general, contemporary, anti-social element driven to its present height by historical development and the zealous co-operation of the Jews themselves, a height at which it must necessarily dissolve itself'. Franz Mehring, *Karl Marx*, trans. Edward Fitzgerald (Ann Arbor: Ann Arbor Press, 1962 [1918]), 72–73.

12 Cited from, of all people, Rosa Luxemburg by Traverso, *The Marxists and the Jewish Question*, 16. For discussion of Marxist responses to Marx see Fischer, *The Socialist Response to Antisemitism in Imperial Germany*, 37–102.

13 Jeffrey Alexander finds 'striking parallels' between representations of Jews in the eighteenth-century Enlightenment and in the nineteenth-century revolutionary tradition. He argues, mistakenly in our view, that Marx's antisemitic stereotypes help explain why Marxist movements subsequently displayed such 'powerful antisemitic overtones'. Alexander, *The Civil Sphere*, 486–488.

14 Bruno Bauer, *The Jewish Problem*, trans. Helen Lederer (Cincinnati: Hebrew Union College, 1958).

15 Karl Marx, 'On the Jewish Question' in Lucio Colletti (ed.), *Karl Marx's Early Writings* (Harmondsworth: Penguin, 1975), 210–241 at 212.

16 Cited in Draper, *Karl Marx's Theory of Revolution, Volume I State and Bureaucracy*, 593.

17 Jean-Paul Sartre was to observe how resistant the antisemitic outlook can be to empirical criticism. In *Antisemite and Jew* (1946) he described antisemitism as a 'passion' neither caused nor refutable by experience: 'The essential thing here is not a "historical fact" but the idea that the agents of history formed for themselves of the Jew'. Sartre observed that there is a sense in which the antisemite can never lose the argument. If we point out that most Jews are not powerful financiers or that most powerful financiers are not Jews, the antisemitic imagination remains no less fixed on the powerful Jewish financier. Marx's refusal to challenge Bauer on empirical grounds may be viewed as being based on similar premises. See Jean-Paul Sartre, *Antisemite and Jew* (New York: Schocken Books, 1965 [1946]), 15.

18 Marx, 'On the Jewish Question', 226. Emphasis in original.

19 Marx, 'On the Jewish Question', 216.

20 Marx, 'On the Jewish Question', 220.

21 Marx, 'On the Jewish Question', 217.

22 Marx, 'On the Jewish Question', 222.

23 Marx, 'On the Jewish Question', 221.

24 Marx, 'On the Jewish Question', 232. Jewish emancipation was later to be followed by antisemitic reactions revoking Jewish emancipation, expelling Jews from a particular territory or eliminating them from the world. This reaction indicates why it remains essential to distinguish between political emancipation and human emancipation.

25 Marx, 'On the Jewish Question', 226.

26 Marx, 'On the Jewish Question', 230.

27 Marx, 'On the Jewish Question', 236–237.

28 Marx and Engels, *The Holy Family or Critique of Critical Criticism*, 98–154.

29 Karl Löwith, *Max Weber and Karl Marx* (London: Routledge, 1993), 106.

30 Georg Lukács, *History and Class Consciousness: Studies in Marxist Dialectics* (Cambridge, MA.: MIT Press, 1971), 178; 184.

31 Karl Marx and Friedrich Engels, 'The Communist Manifesto' in Karl Marx and Friedrich Engels, *Selected Works in One Volume* (London: Lawrence and Wishart, 1970), 31–63, at 38.

32 Marx and Engels, *Communist Manifesto*, 57.

33 Marx, 'On the Jewish Question', 234. Emphasis in original.

3

Antisemitism, critical theory and the ambivalences of Marxism

> Citizens, let us think of the basic principle of the International: Solidarity. Only when we have established this life-giving principle on a sound basis among the numerous workers of all countries will we attain the great final goal which we have set ourselves. (Karl Marx – a speech given following a congress of the First International, 8 September, 1872)[1]

> During my youth I rather leaned toward the prognosis that the Jews of different countries would be assimilated and that the Jewish question would thus disappear in a quasi-automatic fashion. The historical development of the last quarter of a century has not confirmed this perspective … .The Jewish question, I repeat, is indissolubly bound up with the complete emancipation of humanity. (Interview with Leon Trotsky).[2]

Did universalism prepare the way for the antisemitism to come? Our answer may appear equivocal. We do not accept the judgment that the universalism of Enlightenment and the modern revolutionary tradition was simply a failure, but we do recognise that one function of universalism was to represent Jews as the embodiment of the particular and the enemy of humanity. Our conviction, though, is that a universalism that creates its own 'other' ends up as no universalism at all. This was not only, of course, a theoretical question. The reconstruction of the Jewish question had real consequences both for those designated as the other of the universal and for the wider democratic culture. The idea that the multiple problems of modernity could be solved by emptying the world of Jews was taken up with enthusiasm and urgency by antisemitic movements in the latter part of the nineteenth century; it turned out to have extraordinary mobilising power and to appeal to a wide range of political actors. If the legal recognition of Jews was being accomplished in most countries of Western Europe by the end of the 1870s, though not in the East, this was far less true of social recognition of Jews. The emancipation of Jews became an object of multiple resentments, which found political expression in the conceptualisation of the term 'antisemitism' itself as a self-identity and signifier of pride, and in the Europe-wide growth of antisemitic movements and parties.

'Antisemitism' was more than a new name for an old phenomenon; it was also the banner under which diverse hostilities toward Jewish emancipation could be mobilised; a reactive response to the equal treatment of a people not accepted as social equals. It gave a name to the belief that the harmfulness of Jews was made worse by their newfound invisibility and it stood for the restoration of a 'natural' hierarchy in society, in which the subordinate status of Jews would be restored through the enforcement of social and political distinctions. 'Antisemitism' presented the harmfulness of Jews no longer as a transitory and changeable characteristic but as the unalterable quality of their Jewishness. The continuing existence of the Jewish question post-emancipation appeared in the antisemitic imagination as evidence that the corruption of Jews was ineradicable and that the solution to the Jewish question required a harder edge than that of mere 'improvement' through processes of emancipation. Those who prided themselves as antisemites increasingly looked to the hard edges of internal exclusion, external expulsion or *in extremis* extermination.

The rise of antisemitism posed specific problems for emergent Marxist movements after Marx. Marxists generally rejected antisemitism, its essentialist contention that the harm caused by Jews was due to an unalterable Jewishness, and its repressive solutions to the problems it imagined; yet rejection of the 'immoderate' methods of posing and solving the problem did not mean repudiating their views on what is wrong or indeed 'repulsive' about them. Many Marxists were still tempted to *explain* antisemitism in terms of the harm Jews continued to inflict on society and to look to improvement in the behaviour of Jews as at least the first step in the struggle to do away with antisemitism. The description of antisemitism as the 'socialism of fools', usually attributed to the German Marxist August Bebel, was an evocative expression of Marxism's critical response to the rise of the phenomenon but was understood in some quarters as endorsing the view that antisemitism was a kind of socialism, albeit a foolish kind, and that it contained a kernel of truth that was a matter of concern for socialists as well as for antisemites.[3] So while Marxists generally opposed antisemitism, they were also tempted to revive the assumptions of the Jewish question in their very way of understanding and responding to it. This is why Marxists could be as critical of 'philosemites' as of antisemites: while the latter made the problem worse by naturalising Jewish defects and declaring 'no more Jews', the former seemed to obscure the very real and corrosive social harms committed by Jews – especially, as Nietzsche put it, by the 'stock-exchange Jew' on the one hand and the 'ugliness of the recently immigrated Polish and Russian, Hungarian and Galician Jews'[4] on the other. This is also why the self-confidence of Marxism was that its own universalistic principles were incompatible with antisemitism and that the idea of a 'left antisemitism' was an impossible oxymoron, even as they re-affirmed the demand that the Jews must abandon their harmful habits and traits.

Marxism and the Jewish question

We have argued that Marx challenged the view that Jewish emancipation should be made dependent on the condition that Jews abandon their Judaism or on the hope that Jews surrender their identity as Jews as the *quid pro quo* of civic equality. At the same time Marx and Engels confirmed the cosmopolitan credo that the working class has no country: 'The nationality of the worker is neither French, nor English, nor German, it is labour, free slavery, self-huckstering. His government is neither French, nor English, nor German, it is capital'.[5] They seemed to have an optimistic assessment of the empirical state of working-class consciousness when they wrote that 'the great mass of the proletarians are, by their nature, free from national prejudice and their whole disposition and move-ment is essentially humanitarian, anti-nationalist',[6] but the normative conception of human community on which this assessment was based was to look for soli-darities beyond the division of the world into separate nations.[7] They doubtless mistook the wish for the deed when they argued that 'national differences and antagonisms between people are daily more and more vanishing' and that 'national one-sidedness and narrow-mindedness become more and more impos-sible',[8] but their normative concern was to encourage class solidarity both within and across national boundaries – a solidarity imperilled by the appeal of rival nationalisms. In the revolutions of 1848, for example, they were critical of German revolutionaries who resisted the application of the right of national self-determination they claimed for themselves being applied to Danes, Poles, Italians and Czechs, and they led the internationalist section of the left in opposing any such divisive expressions of German nationalism.[9] They recognised the existence of national distinctions but refused to give them privileged status and challenged the dichotomy between 'universal' and 'non-historic' nations ('us' and 'them').[10]

After Marx, however, orthodox Marxism took a nationalist turn, which was fateful in terms of its understanding of the Jewish question. In a context in which Jewish minorities were becoming increasingly vulnerable as the result of the growth of antisemitism and decline of the nation state, international solidarity with Jews became ever more vital. The situation was described thus by the writer, Joseph Roth:

> Every nationality within Austria-Hungary pressed its claim on the basis of its 'territory'. Only the Jews ... had no territory of their own. In Galicia the majority of them were neither Poles nor Ruthenians. However, anti-Semitism was to be found equally among Germans and Czechs, Poles and Ruthenians, Magyars and

Romanians in Transylvania. They managed to refute the proverb that says that when two quarrel, the third is always the winner. The Jews were always the third party and they always lost.[11]

The devaluing of cosmopolitanism and revaluing of the Jewish question combined to disfigure Marxist opposition to antisemitism and in some cases to make its own contribution to the antisemitic canon. The critical stance adopted by Marx and Engels was not entirely abandoned, but repeated attempts were made to replace the critique of nationalism with distinctions between progressive and reactionary forms of nationalism.[12] The most influential of these distinctions was the opposition, endorsed by Lenin, between the 'nationalism of the oppressor' and the 'nationalism of the oppressed'. Lenin's own argument was partly instrumental, advanced in the hope that Marxists might be able to join forces with national resistance to Tsarist imperial rule, and partly empirical, based on the imperial division of the world between colonisers and colonised. The reification of this situated theory into a general doctrine, however, fell to Joseph Stalin who contrived a set of 'mathematical formulae' to determine who constituted a nation and what kind of nation they constituted.[13] One of the effects of this move was to facilitate the old refrain that the Jews were not a nation and could not form one. This paradigm was to find its exemplar in the portrayal of Russia as the universal nation whose own interests corresponded with the general interests of world proletariat and the corresponding portrayal of the Jews as a mere semblance of a nation, in reality 'rootless cosmopolitans'.

Of course, not all Marxists at all times were prepared to abandon Marx's cosmopolitan outlook. Rosa Luxemburg, for example, is well known for stressing the dangers of nationalism: that it created barriers between workers, since it promoted the primacy of national identities and made loyalty to the nation a supreme political value. She maintained that it turned the right of nations to self-determination into a warrant for new states to oppress minorities in their midst – a warrant that was to have serious consequences for Jews, who were minorities in both old and new states.[14] Whereas the Marxist mainstream formally offered uncritical support for a general 'right of nations to self-determination', Luxemburg tempered this doctrine by arguing that while self-determination is a democratic right and essential to struggles against imperial domination, it was being perverted as a thoroughly undemocratic justification for nationalist elites to try to construct homogenous populations with a uniform sense of identity. In the aftermath of the First World War, which Luxemburg had opposed from a broadly cosmopolitan perspective, the newly formed nation states of Central and Eastern Europe manifested just such a drive to homogenise populations and do what was necessary to achieve it, including the exclusion of minorities deemed to belong to other nations or, as in the case of the Jews, to no nation at all.[15] In this context Luxemburg re-affirmed the significance of Marx's *critique* of the

Jewish question at a time when leading Marxists of the German Social Democratic Party effectively came to adopt Bruno Bauer's uncritical absorption by the Jewish question.[16] She demonstrated a better understanding of the dangers antisemitism posed than did orthodox Marxism. Not untypically for Marxists, she was slow to respond to antisemitism at the time of the Dreyfus case; here the initiative was taken more readily by 'reformists' such as Jean Jaures,[17] but by the time of the 1905 revolution she, not unlike Trotsky, recognised that antisemites, far from being winnable for the socialist cause, were its enemies. The failure of the Polish national movement to recognise the dangers posed by antisemitism confirmed Luxemburg in her view that the nationalism they prioritised aligned them effectively with the political Right.[18]

What happened in 1905 was a foretaste of more serious developments that Luxemburg experienced personally in the course of the German revolution of 1918–19. The forces mobilised on the Right to crush the revolution, notably in the *Freikorps* units from which Hitler first began to garner support and from whose ranks Luxemburg's own murderers sprang, had at the heart of their ideology a virulent antisemitism, providing what Geoff Eley has called a 'vocabulary of counter-revolutionary desperation'.[19] The central object of their rage was the 'Judeo-Bolshevik' enemy that had supposedly caused Germany's defeat and had now to be exterminated.[20] Nazism built on the ideological matrix within which the counter-revolutionary Right operated, and provided ways of organising otherwise fractured groupings.[21] How did Marxist movements respond?

Marxism and the final solution

Mainstream Marxism, both in its reformist and revolutionary wings, was opposed to antisemitism and to the antisemitic parties, but did not understand the central role played by antisemitism for the counter-revolution. The temptation to think that there was a 'Jewish question' for society to 'solve' helps explain the reluctance of Marxists, whether Social Democrats or Communists, to make the struggle against antisemitism any kind of priority in spite of the fact that it was being radicalised and pushed to the fore by the Nazis. Inside Germany, neither wing of the Marxist movement appeared to think that antisemitism was central to the Nazi agenda. Both decided it did not call for specific rebuttal and rarely took direct action on this issue.[22] The Social Democrats produced little propaganda to challenge the antisemitic arguments of the Nazis in the last years of the Weimar republic, and the party's attitude appears to have been shaped by fears that it would be over-identified with Jews.[23] Once the Nazis came to power, the underground was instructed not to prioritise the issue on the grounds that antisemitism was more popular than originally estimated and that it would make the work of the resistance more difficult. Klaus Mann, though not himself a member of the Social Democratic Party, spoke for many on the non-Communist left when he too argued in 1941 that 'antisemitism has already played too predominant a part in our propaganda ... it is a dangerous mistake to overemphasise this one particular angle'.[24] The German Communists had a still more problematic record in resisting antisemitism and flirted on several occasions with antisemitic discourse. In 1923 one of its leaders, Ruth Fischer, encouraged Nazi students 'to crush the Jewish capitalists, and hang them from the lamp posts', although she went on to urge them to hang other capitalists too.[25] In the early 1930s, the Communist Party produced leaflets depicting Hitler in league with Jewish capitalists.[26] In the Communist underground, no significant efforts were made to confront antisemitism and it was not until *Kristallnacht* that the party's paper *Die Rote Fahne* gave the issue any prominence.[27] By the time of this state-sponsored violence, Jews had already been systematically removed from the German economy, polity and society.

As the Nazi assault moved beyond the borders of the German nation state to encompass Jews across Europe, and as the threat Jews faced from antisemitism was extended to their survival as members of the human species, Nazi antisemitism acquired what Saul Friedländer has called a 'redemptive' character.[28] It articulated a picture of 'the Jews' as a profound danger, not to Germany alone but to Europe, the Aryan race and humanity. Only through the elimination of the Jews could the 'Jewish question' be 'solved' and humanity made whole again. Nazi antisemitism was a global project, nurtured inside one nation state and then broadened out to eliminate Jews from the world. German Marxists were not alone in failing to respond to the threat posed by Nazi antisemitism, but at a time when the legacy of Marx's critique of the Jewish question was most urgently needed, it was ignored, distorted or squandered. Resistance to the assault on Jews was circumscribed within a frame of reference that did not make what was happening to Jews a priority. For example, when Jews in France were being deported to the camps, the Communist Resistance was still reluctant to make antisemitism a major issue, and no propaganda was produced to highlight what was being done to the Jews in France or elsewhere. Recent research has corroborated that the Communist underground press effectively kept 'total silence ... even when an antisemitic propaganda campaign was launched and even when it directly targeted the resistance' and that 'throughout the occupation, the resistance spared no effort to prove that its members had not signed up to the goal of defending the Jews'.[29] There is compelling evidence that Jewish leadership of Communist resistance was seen as an embarrassment once the Communist parties adopted a super-patriotic line on instruction from Moscow in 1943, the year of the Comintern's official dissolution. The universalism which underpinned the commitment of Jews to the Communist resistance had been tested to the extreme at the time of the Nazi-Soviet pact and led to some Jews leaving the Party in disgust; now it was seen by the Stalinist leadership as such a potent source of disloyalty that they gave orders for Jewish Communist resistance groups in Paris and Toulouse to be betrayed to the Gestapo.[30] None of this is to ignore 'the hand of compassion' offered to Jews by individuals and groups in extremely demanding conditions,[31] but if there was a politics shared by these rescuers, it was informed less by Marxism than by a basic sense of cosmopolitan solidarity with Jews as fellow human beings.

The strategic responses of Marxists organised in Communist Parties were designed and directed from the Soviet Union, even if they were interpreted and applied at the local level. Here the refusal to face up to antisemitism, especially as it became genocidal, was to have disastrous consequences. One effect of the Nazi-Soviet pact of 1939, which allowed Hitler to fight a war of aggression against Poland with Soviet help, was that it was also effectively an arrangement with the most powerful antisemite in the world, which opened the way for the destruction of the largest homeland of Jews in the world.[32] Stalin was well aware of Hitler's antisemitism, as indicated by his decision to fire his Jewish Commissar for Foreign Affairs, Maxim Litvinov, and replace him with the non-Jewish Russian Vyacheslav Molotov, in order to negotiate this agreement. By this time, many Jews had a developed sense of what was in stock for them. Five years of accelerating antisemitic repression in Germany had been followed by shocking violence against Jews in Austria after the *Anschluss* and in Czechoslovakia when it too was annexed. When news of the Molotov-Ribbentrop pact came through to the Zionist World Congress, everyone there understood what it meant for Jews. Chaim Weizmann, leader of the General Zionists, closed the congress with the words: 'Friends, I have only one wish: that we all remain alive'.[33] The secret protocols of the German-Soviet agreement meant that the heartland of world Jewry in East Europe would quickly become the most dangerous place in the world for Jews. When Stalin said that the Molotov-Ribbentrop pact was an alliance 'signed in blood', he signally failed to note that much of the blood would be that of Jews. When large numbers of Jews fell rapidly under Nazi control in 1941, some managed to flee to the Soviet Union, but the Soviet state did not make any plans that took into account the dangers facing the Jewish population across the border.[34] When the Nazis invaded the Soviet Union and the mass shootings of Jews began, the Soviet authorities maintained a systematic and sustained silence about what was happening. For example, the first report that 52,000 Jews had been murdered at Babi Yar was revised down to a figure of 1,000.[35] The war itself was defined in national terms that had nothing to do with the murder of Jews as such. As one Military Council leader put it in 1943, citing Stalin, 'some comrades of Jewish descent believe that this war is being fought to save the Jewish nation. These Jews are mistaken. We fight the Great Patriotic War for the salvation, the freedom and the independence of our homeland led by the Great Russian people'.[36] The practical consequence of this kind of national framing of the conflict with the Nazis was that Jews as Jews were left to fend for themselves. One historian maintains that 'neither from the Soviet state nor from the Party was there a single appeal to underground organisations or the local population to help Soviet Jews'.[37]

After the Holocaust, such indifference evolved into a more familiar pattern. As the Red Army swept west, a Soviet Extraordinary State Commission to Investigate German-Fascist Crimes was set up and given specific instructions to avoid stating that the victims of massacres had been Jews. Along with four other anti-fascist committees, a Jewish anti-Fascist Committee (JAC) had been set up by the Soviet regime in 1942 and had made efforts to publicise for a Western audience what the Nazis were doing to Jews. One of its major projects, published in early 1946, was a detailed record of Nazi crimes, *The Black Book: The Nazi Crime Against the Jewish People*. The fate of this book and the committee is instructive. Even though the regime had carefully vetted membership of the JAC, it was, from the outset, concerned with potential deviations from party orthodoxy on the Jewish question. Drafts of *The Black Book* aroused serious concerns within the regime, precisely because of its emphasis on what was done to Jews, and it was withdrawn in late 1947 from publication on the grounds that it contained 'grave political errors'. All copies were destroyed, along with the typesetting.[38] With the defeat of the Nazis, the JAC had outlived its tactical utility and it was closed down long before other anti-fascist committees. The first victim was its leading activist and spokesman, the playwright Solomon Mikhoels, who was murdered on Stalin's personal orders in January 1948. Other members, some of them die-hard Stalinists, were arrested, tortured, charged and in almost all cases shot.[39] The two decisive charges laid against leaders of the JAC, those of Zionism *and* cosmopolitanism, appear at first sight bizarrely contradictory but what connected them were connotations of disloyalty, lack of patriotism, foreignness and investment in world Jewish conspiracy. The charge of 'Zionism' rested on a selective nationalism that claimed to distinguish between its 'progressive' and 'reactionary' forms and was premised on the disloyalty of Jews conspiring with other Jews to cling to a national identity they should have long foresworn. The phrase 'rootless cosmopolitan Jew' revealed an antipathy to cosmopolitanism, as well as to Jews, that Marx himself did not share.[40] As one loyal Stalinist put it, 'cosmopolitanism is an ideology alien to the workers. Communism has nothing in common with cosmopolitanism, that ideology which is characteristic of representatives of banking firms and international suppliers of weapons and their agents'. Another described cosmopolitanism as 'a false, senseless, strange and incomprehensible phenomenon' and the cosmopolitan as 'a corrupt, unfeeling creature, totally unworthy of being called by the holy name of man'.[41] The dual charges of Zionism and cosmopolitanism formed the basis of a distinctive contribution Stalinised Marxism made to the post-Holocaust repertoire of antisemitism, which was by no means confined to the Soviet Union. In the late 1940s and 1950s, this repertoire was polished in a series of show trials throughout Eastern Europe, most infamously in that of Rudolf Slansky in Eastern Europe, a template for many others.[42] By combining apparent opposites, it re-connected with a long tradition in which Jews could be accused of seemingly contradictory crimes. What connected these charges as new forms of the Jewish question was the representation of Jews both as a transnational group with connections and loyalties which ran across national boundaries, and as a national group with connections and loyalties to a nation state of their own. Either way, Jews could be treated as enemies of the internationalism supposedly embodied in the Soviet state.[43]

Left Marxism, whose centre of gravity was the Trotskyist movement but which also included more libertarian sections of the radical left, was ferociously critical of Stalinised Marxism but was not necessarily able to frame a more coherent understanding of antisemitism. Although it is true that the official position of the Bolsheviks, at least after 1905, was that antisemitism was a fundamentally reactionary force, when it came to combating antisemitism even and perhaps especially during the revolution, the practice was quite different. As Brendon McGeevor has shown, the Red Army itself committed extensive antisemitic violence and was responsible for over 8% of pogroms launched in the Ukraine (Petluira's counter-revolutionary army being responsible for some 40%). Prominent in the slogans pronounced by Red Army units as they fought their way across the Ukraine were calls to 'smash the bourgeoisie, smash the Yids. Long live Soviet power!' When efforts were belatedly made to contain this violence, they were organised not by the party leadership but by former members of the Bund and left-Zionist groups who had come over to the Bolsheviks at that time.[44] They were all later murdered in the Stalinist terror of the 1930s.[45]

It is in this context that we might consider the evolution of Leon Trotsky's understanding of the threat posed by antisemitism. In 1905 Trotsky, like Luxemburg, had seen for himself how antisemitism had been whipped up by the state and how quickly it could mobilise and license the mob to perform acts of extreme violence. This did not prevent him being alarmingly slow, along with other Bolshevik leaders, to react to the antisemitic violence carried out by the Red Army, much of it before he assumed control,[46] but he did have a more acute sense than other Marxists of where it might lead. Norman Geras has suggested that in Trotsky's evocative writing on the pogroms of 1905, we can find the roots of his foreboding in 1938 that with or without war 'the next development of world reaction signifies with certainty the physical extermination of the Jews'.[47] Trotsky's awareness of the genocidal thrust of Nazi antisemitism showed an ability to think critically about the Jewish question in ways that most of his followers were unable to comprehend or sustain.[48]

In the immediate aftermath of the Holocaust Ernest Mandel, who was to become one of the most influential of postwar Trotskyists, acknowledged the challenge posed by the Holocaust before equating the annihilation of the Jews to the postwar expulsion of Germans from Poland and Czechoslovakia: 'the death trains have again begun moving but this time in the opposite direction with a different human freight ... if Hitler constructed the trap for the Jews, it was the Anglo-Americans who sprang it ... the massacre of the Jews is borne equally with Nazism ... by all of imperialism'.[49] The analogy Mandel drew between the Holocaust and the expulsion of Germans, and that between Nazi culpability and imperialism more generally, signalled an unwillingness or inability to think about genocidal antisemitism as such. Mandel was by no means alone in displaying such reluctance. For example, those involved in one of the most intellectually fertile splits from orthodox Trotskyism, grouped around the journal *Socialisme ou Barbarie*, largely ignored the Holocaust.[50] A similar neglect can be observed among the 1968 generation of radical leftists where various versions of Maoism jostled for influence with Trotskyists.[51] The most influential Maoist group in France, *Gauche Prolétarienne*, represented itself as heir to the anti-fascist partisan movement and equated Israel's treatment of the Palestinians to Nazism – an early instance of what has subsequently become a common anti-Zionist thematic. While the *Gauche Prolétarienne* leaders eventually drew back from this position, recognising how easily it could slide into antisemitism, others were less reticent.[52] Some sections of the German radical left also made this equation, leading to a shocking incident on the anniversary of *Kristallnacht* in 1969 when a bomb was planted in a Jewish community centre to draw attention to the ways in which the Jewish state had supposedly become the leading contemporary perpetrator of crimes against humanity or even genocide.[53]

Several decades after his first foray into writing about the Holocaust, Mandel reformulated his position. He now acknowledged that 'there can be no greater injustice than Auschwitz' and described its crimes as 'the worst in history', but he did not explore the centrality of antisemitism to the Nazi project.[54] He argued that the murder of other categories of 'sub-humans' was being planned by the Nazis, and that this was the result of a wider phenomenon – the emergence of a biological hyper-racism that legitimated imperialist exploitation. Mandel's reformulation was part of a growing literature exploring connections between imperialism and genocide, an approach that illuminates important elements of the Nazi project, especially in relation to the killing fields of Eastern Europe,[55] but not the role of antisemitism in the conception and execution of the Holocaust. Jews were not just one of many targets but the primary focus of a movement designed to bring about their total annihilation; Jews were not just colonial subjects exploited in Eastern Europe but were transported there from all over Europe to be tormented, tortured and finally murdered.[56]

Rethinking antisemitism: Adorno, Horkheimer and the *Dialectic of Enlightenment*

While most Marxists had great difficulty in thinking about how Jews could be cast as such an enemy, we have seen that there were exceptions able to develop a more critical and self-critical approach. The most significant contribution to our understanding of antisemitism from within the Marxist tradition, widely conceived, was that developed by Max Horkheimer and Theodor Adorno. Their work on antisemitism may usefully be read as an engagement with and critique of the Marxist orthodoxy. Like the rest of their colleagues in the Frankfurt School, they were initially reluctant to make antisemitism a central focus of their research, and even as they deployed new methods of enquiry – designed to integrate insights from psychoanalysis into a Marxist frame of reference in order to explain how and why the proletariat failed to halt Hitler's rise to power – they eschewed any sustained discussion of antisemitism. Although many of the School's most prominent members were targeted as Jews, they initially preferred to downplay the question of antisemitism and think of themselves at risk predominantly because they were Marxists.[57]

It was not until 1938 that Horkheimer, the acknowledged director of the School, produced its first serious effort to think about antisemitism in his essay 'The Jews and Europe'.[58] The emphasis on Europe in the title was promising in terms of breaking from a strictly national frame of reference but the essay was uneven, as Horkheimer himself later recognised when he decided not to have this essay republished in his collected works. Horkheimer reverted in this essay to an economistic form of Marxism that elsewhere he and his colleagues had gone beyond, seeking to explain what was happening to Jews primarily as an effect of changes in capitalism that made them economically redundant. Identifying Jews as representative of commercial capital, he argued that they were losing their social function as capitalism entered a new phase of development. 'The Jews are stripped of power as agents of circulation, because the modern structure of the economy largely puts that whole sphere out of action … The result is bad for the Jews. They are being run over. Others are the most capable today: the leaders of the new economy and the state'.[59] Horkheimer's article has been criticised for the 'gloating and reproving tone' in which it appears to blame 'rich Jews' for antisemitism and for ignoring the substantial number of German Jews and huge numbers of Jews from further East who were not capitalists of any description, commercial or otherwise.[60] Horkheimer's core assumption, however, was that the attack on Jews was a means to another end and a temporary product of 'the ascendant phase of fascism'.

> At most, antisemitism in Germany is a safety valve for the younger members of the SA. It serves to intimidate the populace by showing that the system will stop at nothing. The pogroms are aimed politically more at the spectators than the Jews.[61]

This line of argument reappeared in the Frankfurt School's major work on the Nazi state, Franz Neumann's *Behemoth* (1942). Neumann insisted, at the very moment that the annihilation programme began in earnest with gas chambers fully operational, that the Nazis would 'never allow a complete extermination of the Jews. The foe cannot and must not disappear'.[62] Antisemitism was not an end in itself but 'only the means to the attainment of the ultimate objective, namely the destruction of free institutions, beliefs and groups ... the testing grounds for universal terrorist methods directed against all those groups and institutions not fully subservient to the Nazi system'. It was to be understood as 'a spearhead of terror'. Like other forms of Nazi ideology, which were 'mere *arcana dominationis*, techniques of domination', Neumann argued that antisemitism was used or discarded to fit the needs of the day.[63] He wrote to Adorno that one could quite properly 'represent National Socialism without attributing to the Jewish problem a central role'.[64] It might be argued that these members of the Frankfurt School, who were by then in American exile and far removed from where the killing was taking place, did not have sufficient information about what was happening to Jews. This is not, however, a compelling explanation, given that Neumann (as well as his close colleague, Herbert Marcuse) was employed as an analyst of Nazi Germany by the US government, which was better informed about the mass killing of Jews than was for many years admitted.[65] It might also be argued that it is unfair to criticise members of the Frankfurt School with the benefit of hindsight given the widespread failure to understand what was happening to Jews.[66] After all, 'even veteran anti-Semites found it hard to imagine that the Nazi regime seriously intended to make the Jewish people extinct'.[67] It is all the more remarkable, then, that Adorno and Horkheimer had the courage to re-think this approach to understanding antisemitism and the assumptions of the Jewish question running through it.

Adorno had already begun to have premonitions about what the Nazis might be intending. As one commentator has put it, Adorno 'seems to have become more sensitive to the approaching storm than others in the group'.[68] In February 1938, in a letter to Horkheimer, he raised the possibility of gassing and pointed to the acute vulnerability of Jews under existing national conditions: 'There can be scarcely any room for doubt that the remaining Jews in Germany will be wiped out; for as the dispossessed, no country in the world will grant them admission'.[69] What was being done to Jews was moving closer to the centre of their concerns. In August 1940 Adorno wrote to Horkheimer: 'under the influence of the latest news from Germany ... I cannot stop thinking about the Jews any more. It often seems to me that everything that we used to see from the point of view of the proletariat has been concentrated with frightful force upon the Jews ... who are now at the opposite pole to the concentration of power'.[70] The antisemitism question was no longer a marginal issue. As Adorno put it, 'antisemitism is today really the central injustice, and our form of physiognomy must attend to the world where it shows its face at its most gruesome'.[71] This change of focus required radical rethinking. The elimination of a whole group of people, the attempt to remove them not only from one geographical area but also from the human world, raised fundamental questions about civilisation, the direction of historical development and the prospects for humanity itself. In 1942 Horkheimer wrote:

> whoever accuses the Jews today aims straight at humanity itself. The Jews have become the martyrs of civilisation ... To protect the Jews has come to be a symbol of everything mankind stands for ... The Jews have been made what the Nazis always pretended they were – the focal point of world history.[72]

To understand how and why this group became the object of such dedicated destructive intent required a major re-assessment, not only of antisemitism but also of the Marxist tradition itself. Horkheimer came to realise, as he wrote to Marcuse, that 'the problem of antisemitism is much more complicated than I thought' and that to understand it, one had to connect economic and political factors with anthropological ones, to 'show these factors in their constant inter-connection and describe how they permeate each other'.[73]

This major project was to be conducted at several levels. Horkheimer and Adorno began by sketching out a 'genealogy' of antisemitism.[74] In a wide-ranging 1941 research proposal they suggested that this would require the study *inter alia* of the First Crusade, the Albigensian heresy, Jew-baiting in twelfth- and thirteenth-century England, the Reformation, the French Revolution, the German war of resistance to Napoleon, and political antisemitism in the nine-teenth and twentieth centuries![75] This comprehensive historical study was to be accompanied by a series of research projects into contemporary antisemitism, including in the United States where they had been based since leaving Germany. Working with Jewish organisations such as the American Jewish Committee and the Jewish Labour Committee, they developed several research proposals on antisemitism that involved collaboration with a wide range of scholars.[76] At the same time, Horkheimer and Adorno fundamentally recast their approach to antisemitism as part of a larger re-appraisal of the Enlightenment legacy in their *Dialectic of Enlightenment*, the last chapter of which was devoted to analysing 'the elements of antisemitism' and 'the limits of Enlightenment' antisemitism represented.[77] This was the culmination of an argument they were working out in the book, to explore how it was that the development of civilisation regressed into the endeavour of a modern state (in one of the most advanced societies in the world) to murder a whole category of people and erase the idea of humanity.

One source of inspiration for this project was located within the Marxist tradi-tion. At the outset of the First World War, when Rosa Luxemburg was resisting the nationalism to which many of her peers on both sides of the conflict had succumbed, she recalled Engels' warning that modern civilisation might regress into barbarism. In contemplating such a possibility, Luxemburg sketched out what barbarism might mean: 'the destruction of all culture ... depopulation, desolation, degeneration, a vast cemetery'.[78] The example she drew on was that of the genocide of Armenians, committed by one of the warring parties during the First World War, the Ottoman regime, with the connivance of the German state.[79] This genocide provided not only a precedent but an inspiration to Nazis, as Hitler made explicit when he told his generals that 'no one now remembers the Armenians' (meaning, as Omer Bartov acidly comments, that he and his audience did remember all too well).[80] The 'final solution to the Jewish question' arguably went beyond even what was done to the Armenians: the aim was not 'only' deportation, plunder and mass murder in one region under the cover of war, but to hunt Jews down across Europe and the world, including of course Palestine, and annihilate the whole lot.[81]

Why were Jews singled out for extermination? The final chapter of *Dialectic of Enlightenment* did not come to a conclusion and was arguably not intended to do so. The title of the chapter 'Elements of antisemitism' suggested that no comprehensive explanation was possible or desirable. The concern of Horkheimer and Adorno was not to provide the kind of determinist account one finds in orthodox Marxism, which would mean that what happened *had* to happen, but to keep history open, i.e. to resist closure and avoid final conclusions. It was not necessarily a weakness that there was no clear hierarchy among the 'elements' they discussed.[82] Their approach was rather an attempt to understand how the different elements of antisemitism were combined and recombined, and why the appearance of one element did not necessarily entail the disappearance of another.[83] As the use of the term 'dialectic' in the book title suggests, older elements could be preserved and subsumed within the new framework. This is what Horkheimer and Adorno argued, for example, in the case of religious forms of antisemitism, which were variously 'channelled' or 'converted' into secular forms.[84] At various points, Horkheimer and Adorno appear to regress to earlier positions mainstreamed within Marxism: sometimes to economic reductionism, sometimes to holding Jews responsible for their own predicament, sometimes to the suggestion that Jews might be interchangeable with any other group. No thinkers easily break free from initial assumptions, and the difficulties of understanding posed by what was happening to Jews were so acute that it was tempting to resort to familiar nostrums. What is striking about this work is how much rethinking of their original presuppositions was nonetheless involved and how this process of rethinking appears, as it were, on the page itself.

Adorno and Horkheimer began with a statement of recognition of the gravity of the problem. The acute danger facing Jews is that they have been 'branded as absolute evil by those who are absolutely evil ... marked out as the absolute object of domination pure and simple ... who must be wiped from the face of the earth'.[85] Although they briefly reverted to Horkheimer's original argument

that workers were the 'ultimate target', they took up the core issue raised in
Marx's critique of Bauer, the connection between Enlightenment and the Jewish
question, now reformulated in terms of the connection between liberalism and
antisemitism. They maintained that liberalism appeared fundamentally opposed
to Nazi antisemitism but could not provide the basis for a coherent response as
long as it continued to assume that Jews had to give up something of their
Judaism as the condition of becoming part of civilised society. To be sure,
Horkheimer and Adorno recognised that not all liberals pathologise Jewishness,
any more than all Enlightenment thinkers singled out Judaism as uniquely toxic,
but they argued that assimilationist tendencies in liberalism were based on the
assumption that the society into which Jews were supposed to assimilate possessed a unity and harmony that could only be disrupted by the persistence of
a distinct and harmful Jewish identity. The apprehension they expressed is that
the homogenising sense of national identity into which liberalism was drawn
was moving inexorably in racist and antisemitic directions. Lurking within the
liberal tradition, Horkheimer and Adorno discerned a potential for prejudice
and persecution which found expression in the exclusion of Jews from the
national community: 'The harmony of society which the liberal Jews believed in
turned against them in the form of the harmony of a national community'.[86]
The mistake was to think that 'antisemitism would distort that order which in
reality cannot exist without distorting men. The persecution of the Jews, like any
other form of persecution, is inseparable from that system of order'.[87]

To be sure, Horkheimer and Adorno were tempted to explain antisemitism,
as Horkheimer had done in 1938, as a 'diversion' by the 'ruling clique' that
appealed to 'covetous mobs', but they understood that this scapegoat approach
cannot explain why Jews were targeted.[88] What was needed was the recognition
of antisemitism as 'deep-rooted in civilisation … a deeply imprinted schema,
a ritual of civilisation' itself'.[89] They returned to the economic argument that
insofar as Jews were confined to commercial and financial forms of capital, it
was because they were 'still largely denied access to the origins of surplus value',
but called for an understanding of how and why Jews are made into 'scapegoats
not only for individual manoeuvres and machinations but in a broader sense,
inasmuch as the injustice of the whole class is attributed to them'. Involved here
was what Horkheimer and Adorno called the 'concealment of domination in pro-
duction … an ideology cloaking the real nature of the labour contract'.[90] If what
is concealed is represented as the fault of the Jews, antisemitism must play a key
role in the legitimation of capitalism. At times Horkheimer and Adorno inverted
the whole imagery of Jewish particularism characteristic of the Jewish question,
declaring for instance that Jews have always been 'colonisers for progress': 'From
the time when, in their capacity as merchants they helped to spread Roman civilisation throughout Gentile Europe, they were the representatives – in harmony

with their patriarchal religion – of municipal, bourgeois and finally industrial conditions'. This was more than an economic role. Jews helped develop core ethical principles of the modern world only to discover that these principles did not apply to them: 'Those who proclaimed individualism, abstract justice and the notion of the person are now degraded to the condition of a species ... they are never allowed to enjoy freely the civil rights which should allow them human dignity'.[91] The idea that Jews need to be civilised is turned on its head. That civilisation can turn on Jews in the name of progress can only mean there is something wrong with 'civilisation' and 'progress'.

Part of this interrogation involved rethinking the relationship of antisemitism to Christianity. Horkheimer and Adorno saw it as a mistake to think that the religious hostility that lay behind two thousand years of persecution of Jews had simply disappeared. Religion had been 'subsumed and not abolished' and a distinctively religious antisemitism remained available as a resource, even if secular antisemitism claimed to ignore religious considerations. That some did not ignore them was evident within the German Church in which, as they tartly observed, antisemitism was 'all that the German Christians have retained from the religion of love'.[92] The Enlightenment orthodoxy generally reserved greater scorn for Judaism than for Christianity: it saw Christianity as more universalistic than Judaism, since the Christian word of God was for all humanity while Judaism was for the chosen people alone, and as more imbued with the spirit of self-reflection, since it did not just follow the letter of the law: 'Do not be afraid; the Law is secondary to faith'.[93] Horkheimer and Adorno responded that in one respect Christianity represented a 'regression behind Judaism': beneath its apparently more enlightened version of monotheism there was a return to a primitive view of the world, which re-imported the pagan 'man-God' based on the assumption that 'the man Jesus has become God'. The temptation Adorno and Horkheimer found within Christian universalism was to represent the continued existence of Judaism as an obstacle to human progress – a stubborn problem that would not go away. They traced 'the religious origin of antisemitism' back to the notion that 'the adherents of the religion of the Father are hated by those who support the religion of the Son – hated as those who know better'.[94]

Horkheimer and Adorno picked up on the wing of Enlightenment and then of socialism that sought to make a decisive break from the Jewish question. Antisemitism has to do with what is projected onto Jews, not with the conduct of Jews themselves. What was needed was an understanding of 'the mental energy harnessed by antisemitism',[95] which they identified with projection of what is intolerable inside oneself onto Jews: 'Antisemitism is self-hatred, the bad conscience of the parasite'.[96] This is why Horkheimer and Adorno distinguished between projection as such, which is necessary to all perception based on the 'distinction between within and without' and on the possibility of 'self-awareness and the conscience',[97] and false projection characterised by absence of reflection:

> since he [the antisemite] no longer reflects on the object, he ceases to reflect upon himself ... Instead of the voice of conscience, he hears other voices; instead of examining himself in order to decipher the protocol of its own lust for power, [he] attributes the 'Protocols of the Elders of Zion' to others ... It [false projection] invests the world boundlessly with its own content.[98]

The content of antisemitism is filled with 'fantasies of Jewish crimes, infanticide and sadistic excess, poisoning of the nation and international conspiracy'. While these fantasies go back a long way, what was new to the Nazi period was their 'practical implementation' which 'goes beyond the evil content of the projection'.[99] Nazism was a 'special case of paranoiac delusion'.[100] Common to all paranoiacs is confusion between the inner and the outer world: 'Impulses which the subject will not admit as his own even though they are most assuredly so, are attributed to the object – the prospective victim'. In genocidal antisemitism 'this behaviour is made political: the object of the illness is deemed true to reality; and the mad system becomes the reasonable norm in the world'.[101] While the 'solitary paranoiac' interprets the world 'in a private manner which is shared by no one and therefore appears totally mad', among Nazis 'illness is socialised ... Projecting their madness, they see conspiracy ... everywhere'.[102] Their project is to eliminate opposition through violence, first against individuals and then against collectivities through a 'carefully conceived strategy of extermination'.[103] Violence binds the community as a racialised nation: 'the normal member of society dispels his own paranoia by participation in the collective form and clings passionately to the objectivised, collective and confirmed forms of delusion'.[104] The corollary of Nazi paranoia is the desire for omnipotence: 'The antisemites try to realise their negative absolute by their own power, and change the world into the hell which they always thought it was'.[105] The elimination of difference becomes a 'substitute for omnipotence. It is as though the serpent who said to the first men "you will be as God" had redeemed its promise in the paranoiac. He makes everything in his own image. ... His will permeates the universe'. The desire for total domination is 'the mocking image of divine power ... like the devil ... driven by compulsion ... If it is said that divine power attracts creation, satanic power likewise draws everything into its own impotence. This is the secret of its domination'.[106] 'The Jews' of antisemitic paranoia are thought to

> lag behind civilisation and yet to be too far ahead of it: they are both clever and stupid, similar and dissimilar. They are declared guilty of something which they ... were the first to overcome: the lure of base instincts, reversion to animality ... the service of images. Because they invented the concept of kosher meat, they are

persecuted as swine. The antisemites make themselves the executors of the Old Testament: they want the Jews who have eaten of the tree of knowledge to return unto dust.[107]

The return of the Jews, who were in fact 'defenceless victims', unto dust found its juridical protection 'in the name of the legal principle of sovereign national rights, which tolerates any act of violence in another country'.[108] There appeared to be nothing to stop the Nazis going ahead with their paranoid projection: to 'forcibly make over [the Jews] into a physical semblance of that image of death and destruction', which they with their 'fantasies of Jewish crimes' projected onto them.[109]

Contributions of critical theory to the critique of the Jewish question

Adorno and Horkheimer's analysis of the elements of antisemitism reveals that it was, as Horkheimer already sensed, a more complicated question than they previously thought. To think about it, they had to break radically from the assumptions of the Jewish question in all its variants, including those of orthodox Marxism, and reconstruct its critique in the context of its 'final solution'. The further question that arose for Horkheimer and Adorno was what would happen to antisemitism after the Holocaust, once there was general recognition of the barbarism it represented. Would such recognition designate the disappearance of antisemitism? They feared this might not be the case. Although Nazi Germany was militarily defeated and the Holocaust was stopped before the 'final solution' was fully final, there could be no guarantee that antisemitism would simply disappear from the social and political landscape. The dissection of different elements of antisemitism in *Dialectic of Enlightenment* suggests that it was possible for them to be added to and recombined in new ways as long as there was a Jewish question to consider. In defeated Germany, they found evidence of a persisting Jewish question being rearticulated in new ways. In a study conducted in 1950–1951, when they had returned to Germany, they maintained that in some quarters antisemitism had been reworked and protected behind a wall of sophisticated defence mechanisms, which turned the perpetrator into victim and victim into perpetrator.[110] They saw this inversion as a distinctive feature of post-Holocaust antisemitism. The defensive move to accuse the Jews of their own crimes revealed a reluctance to think about what was done to Jews or about the return of antisemitism. Adorno deployed the term 'secondary antisemitism' to conceptualise a prejudice he found extant among some Germans, that 'the Jews' were culpable of exploiting German guilt over the Holocaust. He argued that the existence of secondary antisemitism in postwar Germany expressed a failure to see the difference between merely mastering the Nazi past (*Vergangenheitsbewaltingung*) and working through it (*Aufarbeitung der Vergangenheit*); between a superficial break with Nazi rule and the greater challenge of reflecting on the roots of antisemitism in the modern age.

On the radical left, there was much justified criticism of the continuing presence of former Nazis in German society and the German state and of the reluctance of older generations to examine what had been done to Jews. Consumed by the idea that fascism had not been definitively vanquished, however, a way of thinking developed within the left that came to the reductive judgment that there was in the end no significant difference between liberal democracy and Nazism. In the 1960s, in the course of rightful protests against the Vietnam War, this critique was extended to the United States and the West more generally. The place of Israel in this frame of reference was particularly striking. The Jewish nation came to be seen as the archetypal perpetrator of imperialist crimes – accused of committing the same crimes against the Palestinians as the Nazis had committed against the Jews. The Jews became the new Nazis. Fortunately, this was not the only response within the Marxist left but it set the scene of a reconfiguring of the Jewish question. It was in part because Adorno and Horkheimer had come to reject this frame of reference that they were forced to part ways with a student movement that they had inspired.[111]

Adorno and Horkheimer understood that antisemitism is not invariant but an evolving social phenomenon, that its various elements can be combined and recombined in different settings, that it is not the problem of one nation only but for humanity itself, and that it casts a very dark shadow on any claim that History is proceeding 'inevitably' or even 'dialectically' in a progressive direction.[112] They revived an alternative tradition to face up to antisemitism not as a 'niche issue' or 'interlude' (*zwischenspiel*), as Adorno put it, but as a deeply rooted problem of humanity, and to see the 'final solution' as a catastrophe whose meaning was far from exhausted.[113] They drew on a critique of the Jewish question that was formative for Marx but marginal to the mainstreams of Marxism.

The existence of a body of Enlightenment universalism that confronts the idea of a 'Jewish question' is too often glossed over. It was a great strength of critical theory both to re-affirm the validity of universalism as a principle, and to insist that it loses all meaning when set in opposition to the particular. Those approaches to Enlightenment that do not address its internal relation to antisemitism are as flawed as those that do not address its internal relation to slavery, for they both erase human suffering from the history of political thought. This is not to endorse a counter-current that knows how to condemn universalism for its exclusionary relation to Jews and slaves but remains oblivious to its humanist worth.

The question Horkheimer and Adorno posed in the shadow of catastrophe was 'whether the ruled can see and control themselves in the face of absolute madness and call a halt to it'. Their answer was conditional: 'If thought is liberated from domination and if violence is abolished, the long absent idea is liable to develop that Jews too are human beings. This development would represent the step out of an antisemitic society … and into the human society … The Jewish question would then be the turning point of history'.[114] We should hold firm to the idea that the Jewish question may have been such a turning point in the modern world, as we move to our next chapter on the Jewish writings of Hannah Arendt and the peculiar difficulties the Jewish question has posed for Jews themselves.

Notes

1 Karl Marx – a speech given following a congress of the First International, 8 September, 1872. Karl Marx, *The First International and After*, ed. David Fernbach (New York: Vintage), 325.

2 From an interview given by Leon Trotsky to correspondents of the Jewish press upon his arrival in Mexico. Republished in *Fourth International* Vol. VI, No. 12 (Whole No. 61), December 1945, https://www.marxists.org/archive/trotsky/1940/xx/jewish.htm (accessed 2 October 2015).

3 This formulation is often attributed to August Bebel, the leader of the German Social Democratic Party for many years, although it has been suggested that the term originated not with him but with an Austrian liberal, Ferdinand Kronawetter. See Jack Jacobs, *On Socialist and 'The Jewish Question' After Marx* (New York: New York University Press, 1992), ch. 2 'Eduard Bernstein: After All. A German Jew'. It seems that Bebel was himself not entirely happy with the use of the term socialism in this context. In an interview conducted with Hermann Bahr in 1894, he expressed reservations about this formulation, noting that if some workers encountered Jews as small capitalists, most Jews were, especially in the East, workers or peasants, and most Germans knew nothing about Jews at all. Hermann Bahr, 'Der Antisemitismus – Ein Internationales Interview' in Claus Pias (ed.), *Hermann Bahr: Kritische Schriften*, vol. 3, 21–24, www.univie.ac.at/bahr/node/83302 (accessed 15 December 2015). We are grateful to Olaf Kistenmacher for alerting us to this caveat.

4 See Robert C. Holub, *Nietzsche's Jewish Problem: Between Anti-Semitism and Anti-Judaism* (Princeton: Princeton University Press, 2016), 118–123.

5 Karl Marx and Friedrich Engels, 'Critique of List' in *Collected Works*, vol. 4 (London: Lawrence and Wishart, 1975 [1845]), 280. The significance for Marx's cosmopolitanism of this critique of List, as the leading contemporary exponent of nationalism in economic theory, is brought out well by Roman Szporluk in his *Communism and Nationalism: Karl Marx versus Friedrich List* (New York: Oxford University Press 1988). John Hall tellingly describes List as 'the Marx of nationalism' in *The State of the Nation: Ernest Gellner and the Theory of Nationalism* (Cambridge: Cambridge University Press), 31.

6 Friedrich Engels, 'The Festival of Nations in London' in Marx and Engels *Collected Works*, vol. 6 (London: Lawrence and Wishart, 1976 [1845]), 6.

7 See Erica Benner, *Really Existing Nationalisms: A Post-Communist View from Marx and Engels* (Oxford: Oxford University Press 1995), 11.

8 Marx and Engels, 'The Communist Manifesto' in Marx and Engels *Collected Works*, vol. 6 (London: Lawrence and Wishart, 1976 [1848]), 483.

9 Dieter Langeswiehe, 'Germany and the National Question' in John Breuilly (ed.), *The State of Germany: The National Idea in the Making, Unmaking and Remaking* (London: Longman, 1992).

10 Michael Hughes, *Nationalism and Society: Germany 1800–1945* (London: Edward Arnold, 1988). They were, of course, well aware that this was not only a 'German' temptation and, as Gilbert Achcar has noted, they were sharply critical of similar tendencies in France. Gilbert Achcar, *Marxism* (London: Saqi Books, 2013), 112. Engels took Louis Blanc to task, for example, for seeming to demand 'all others to become Frenchmen'. Friedrich Engels, 'The Reform Movement in France: The Banquet of Dijon' in Karl Marx and Friedrich Engels, *Collected Works*, vol. 6 (London: Lawrence and Wishart, 1976 [1847]), 399.

11 Joseph Roth, *The Wandering Jews*, trans. Michael Hoffman (New York: W.W. Norton and Co, 2001).

12 For a critical survey of various such attempts, albeit written from a perspective rather different to our own, see Ephraim Nimni, *Marxism and Nationalism: Theoretical Origins of the Political Crisis* (London: Pluto Press, 1991).

13 Enzo Traverso, *The Marxists and the Jewish Question* (New York: Humanities Press, 1994), 135.

14 For a collection of her oft-derided views on nationalism, see Rosa Luxemburg, *The National Question*, ed. Horace B. Davis (New York: Monthly Review Press, 1976). See also Anita Shelton, 'Rosa Luxemburg and the National Question', *East European Quarterly*, 21 (3), 1987: 297–303.

15 For various such efforts, see Rogers Brubaker, *Nationalism and the National Question in the New Europe* (Cambridge: Cambridge University Press, 1996). Hannah Arendt was particularly clear on the dangers such moves posed to Jews and other minorities in *Origins*.

16 On Luxemburg's retrieval of Marx's arguments, see Fischer, *The Socialist Response to Antisemitism*, 221–222.

17 In his defence of Dreyfus, Jean Jaurès too at times located his arguments within the prevailing Marxist framework, arguing that 'even for the benefit of a Jew, we have the right to demand legal guarantees' and even assuring one audience that he understood their antisemitism: 'Yes, down with the Jews! But down with the Christians who are Jews'. Cited in Ruth Harris, *Dreyfus: Politics, Emotion, and the Scandal of the Century* (New York: Metropolitan Books, 2010), 261. It was far from the case that those who defended Dreyfus were animated by their opposition to antisemitism; in fact, many committed Dreyfusards ended up collaborating enthusiastically with the Vichy regime. See Simone Epstein, *Les Dreyfusards sous l'Occupation* (Paris: Albin Michel, 2007).

18 For a careful discussion of a particularly instructive episode which attracted Luxemburg's attention at this time, see Fischer, *The Socialist Response to Antisemitism*, 218–220.

19 Geoff Eley, 'What Are the Contexts for German Antisemitism? Some Thoughts on the Origins of Nazism, 1800–1945' in Jonathan Frankel (ed.), *Studies in Contemporary Jewry, XII: The Fate of the European Jews, 1939–1945* (New York and Oxford: Oxford University Press, 1997), 125.

20 The need to exterminate the 'Jewish enemy', if another defeat was to be avoided, was a constant theme of Nazi propaganda which grew in intensity as the Second World War progressed. See Jeffrey Herf, *Nazi Propaganda for the Arab World* (New Haven, Conn.: Yale University Press, 2010). It found a willing audience in those who carried out the 'final solution'. Omer Bartov has demonstrated a clear connection between the antisemitic exterminatory fantasies of the *Freikorps* and those soldiers who were extensively involved in mass killing of Jews in the East. Both 'came to view their criminal actions … as exacting a just and necessary retribution for past defeats and humiliations … and thereby ensuring the final victory [over Judeo-Bolshevism]' and could 'portray mass killing of civilians [Jews] as a glorious and final reckoning with foes who had been poised to inflict untold barbarities on the German *Volk*'. Omer Bartov, *Mirrors of Destruction: War, Genocide, and Modern Identity* (New York: Oxford University Press, 2000), 28. Saul Friedländer (2007) has explained in his magisterial *Nazi Germany and the Jews* (New York: HarperCollins, 1997) that the Judeo element in the Judeo-Bolshevik couplet came first and had clear primacy.

21 Lee McGowan, 'The Extreme Right' in Panikos Panayi (ed.), *Weimar and Nazi Germany: Continuities and Discontinuities* (London: Longman, 2001), 246–272.

22 Donald Niewyk, *Socialist, Anti-Semite and Jew: German Social Democracy Confronts the Problem of Anti-Semitism, 1918–1933* (Baton Rouge: Louisiana State, 1971).

23 David Bankier, 'German Social Democrats and the Jewish Question' in David Bankier (ed.), *Probing the Depths of German Anti-Semitism: German Society and the Persecution of the Jews 1933–1941* (Oxford: Berghahn, 2000), 511–532.

24 Cited in Bankier, 'German Social Democrats', 521.

25 Cited in Davis William Daycock, *The KPD and the NSDAP: A Study of the Relationship between Political Extremes in Weimar Germany, 1923–1933*, PhD thesis (London School of Economics, 1980).

26 Timothy Brown, *Weimar Radicals: Nazis and Communists Between Authenticity and Performance* (New York: Berghahn, 2009), 104.

27 Jeffrey Herf, 'German Communism, the Discourse of "Anti-Fascist" Resistance and the Jewish Catastrophe' in Michael Geyer and John W. Boyer (eds.), *Resistance in the Third Reich* (Chicago: Chicago University Press, 1994), 257–294.

28 Saul Friedlander, *Nazi Germany and the Jews 1939–45: The Years of Extermination* (London: Weidenfeld and Nicolson, 2007), xviii.

29 Daniel Blatman and Renée Poznanski, 'Jews and their Social Environment: Perspectives from the Underground Press in Poland and France' in Beata Kosmala and Georgi Verbeeck (eds.), *Facing the Catastrophe: Jews and non-Jews in Europe during World War Two* (Oxford: Berg, 2011), 159–228, at 201.

30 On this shocking episode, see the careful investigation by Maurice Rajsfus, *L'An Prochain la Révolution: Les Communistes Juifs Immigrés dans la Tourmente Stalinienne 1930–45* (Paris: Editions Mazarine, 1985), 197–226.

31 Karen Monroe, *The Hand of Compassion: Portraits of Moral Choice During the Holocaust* (Princeton, NJ: Princeton University Press, 2004).

32 Timothy Snyder, *Black Earth: The Holocaust as History and Warning* (New York: Tim Duggan Books, 2015), 103.

33 Cited in Snyder, *Black Earth*, 103.

34 Ben-Cion Pinchuk, 'Was There a Soviet Policy for Evacuating the Jews? The Case of the Annexed Territories', *Slavic Review*, 39, 1, 1980, 44–55.

35 Arno Lustiger, *Stalin and the Jews: The Red Book: The Tragedy of the Jewish Anti-Fascist Committee and the Soviet Jews* (New York: Enigma, 2003), 106.

36 Lustiger, *Stalin and the Jews*, 108.

37 Quoted in Harvey Asher, 'The Soviet Union, the Holocaust and Auschwitz' in Michael David-Fox, Peter Holquist and Alexander M. Martin (eds.), *The Holocaust in the East: Local Perpetrators and Soviet Responses* (Pittsburg: University of Pittsburg Press, 2014), 29–50, at 44.

38 Zvi Gitelman, 'Politics and the Historiography of the Holocaust in the Soviet Union' in Zvi Gitelman (ed.), *Bitter Legacy: Confronting the Holocaust in the USSR* (Bloomington: Indian University Press, 1997), 19.

39 Joshua Rubenstein and Vladimir P. Naumov, *Stalin's Secret Pogrom: The Postwar Inquisition of the Jewish Anti-Fascist Committee* (New Haven: Yale University Press, 2001).

40 Gilbert Achcar argues persuasively that the antipathy to cosmopolitanism found within Marxist circles was not shared by Marx or Engels themselves, who were inclined to use the term positively rather than pejoratively. Achcar, *Marxism*, 123. Michael Löwy, similarly, claims that 'there is no doubt that Engels considered himself to be a consistent cosmopolitan'. Michael Löwy, *Fatherland or Mother Earth? Essays on the National Question* (London: Sterling, Va.: Pluto Press with the International Institute for Research and Education 1998), 8.

41 Quoted in Benjamin Pinkus and Jonathan Frankel. *The Soviet Union and the Jews, 1948–67* (Cambridge: Cambridge University Press, 1984), 152 and 154.

42 Of the 14 defendants singled out in the Slansky trial, the largest of all the purge trials held in this period, at least 11 were Jews. See Tomas Snigeon, *Vanished History: The Holocaust in Czech and Slovak Political Culture* (Oxford: Berghahn, 2014), 61. Antisemitism had also been a feature of the Moscow trials of the late 1930s, where it formed a crucial 'subtext', and even before, in the context of actions taken against Trotsky in the 1920s. See Vadim Rogovin, *1937: Stalin's Year of Terror* (Sheffield: Mehring, 1998), 154. On the antisemitic aspect of the campaign against Trotsky in the 1920s, see Bernard Wasserstein, *On the Eve: The Jews of Europe Before the Second World War* (New York: Simon and Schuster, 2012), 64.

43 See, for example, Orlando Figes, *The Whisperers: Private Life in Stalin's Russia* (London; New York: Allen Books, 2007), 454, and Frank Gruner, ' "Russia's Battle Against the Foreign": The Anti-Cosmopolitanism Paradigm in Russian and Soviet Ideology' in Michael L. Miller and Scott Ury (eds.), *Cosmopolitanism, Nationalism and the Jews of East Central Europe* (London: Routledge), 109–136.

44 For a detailed study of this Red Army violence, see the PhD by Brendon McGeevor, *A Historical Sociology of the Bolshevik Response to Antisemitism and Pogromist Violence During the Russian Revolution* (Glasgow University, 2015).

45 The murder of Jews *as* Jews was part (though not the central part) of Stalin's paranoia about some nationalities as sources of disloyalty to the Soviet Union at this time. On the murderous consequences of this paranoia for Jews as well as others (notably Poles), see Timothy Snyder, *Bloodlands: Europe Between Hitler and Stalin* (London: Bodley Head, 2010). This paranoia was not of course grounded in any cosmopolitan vision, nor was it at all incompatible with what was very soon to be an overt embrace of Russian patriotism in the 'Great Patriotic War' against Nazi Germany.

46 McGeevor argues that it was not possible for the party leadership to control much of what was going on at the base. Many of those who fought in the Red Army were peasant partisans who brought with them a long-standing and virulent antisemitism. Bolshevik commissars who tried to do something to contain the antisemitic violence (when they dared, which was rarely) were brushed aside.

47 Norman Geras, *The Contract of Mutual Indifference; Political Philosophy After the Holocaust*: (London: Verso, 1998), 158–159; the quotation (cited in Geras, 139) is from Trotsky, *On the Jewish Question* (New York: Pathfinder Press, 1970), 29. We are not aware of any other Marxist, or indeed any other prominent political or social theorist, who made such an acute diagnosis of what was looming at this time.

48 In a set of detailed interviews with Trotskyists in France, where the movement was most influential, Jean Birnbaum found an 'almost perfect identity of the revolutionary position … before and after the bloody caesura', an insistence as a matter of principle on speaking as little as possible about antisemitism, and on rejecting anything which drew attention to the particular fate of Jews. *Leur Jeunesse et la Notre: L'Espérance Révolutionnaire au Fil des Générations* (Paris: Stock, 2005), 345. See, in particular, ch. 4 'Sois Juif et Tais-toi! L'Universalisme a Corps Perdu', 303–358.

49 Ernest Mandel, 'The Jewish Question since World War Two' republished in www.workersliberty.org/node/8914 [1946] (accessed 6 September 2014), 2; 3.

50 Concerning the dearth of Marxist scholarship on the Holocaust, see Philippe Reynaud, *L'Extrême Gauche Plurielle* (Paris: Editions Perrin, 2010) and Philippe Gottraux, *Socialisme ou Barbarie: Un Engagement Politique et Intellectuel dans la France de l'Après-Guerre* (Lausanne: Payot-Lausanne 1997). An exception is Arno Mayer's *Why did the Heavens Not Darken?* published by the radical publishing house Verso in 1988. This work, however, specifically sets out to downplay the role of antisemitism in the Holocaust.

51 Yair Auron, *Les Juifs et l'Extrême Gauche en Mai 68: Une Génération Marquée par la Shoah* (Paris: Albin Michel, 1998).

52 See Hervé Hamon and Patrick Rotman, *Génération: Volume 2, Les Années de Poudre* (Paris: Le Seuil 1988). For an interesting reflection by a member of the *Gauche Prolétarienne* on how and why antisemitism was systematically ignored, see Jean-Claude Milner *L'Arrogance du Présent: Regards sur une Décennie, 1965–1975* (Paris: Grasset, 2009) ch. 8, 'Le Juif de Révolution'. The leader of *Gauche Prolétarienne*, Benny Lévy, came to see an unwillingness on the left to think about antisemitism as a reason why it was prone to adopt unreflective pro-Palestinian positions. Lévy, who later turned to orthodox Judaism after a prolonged engagement with the work of Emmanuel Lévinas, was a major if contested influence on Jean-Paul Sartre, who shielded Lévy from Gaullist persecution. Lévy may have helped fortify Sartre's

determined refusal to abandon his deep concern with antisemitism and his under-standing of Israel as a refuge for Jews after the Holocaust. Many on the left were discomfited by this position of Sartre's and sought to blame Lévy, a charge rebutted convincingly by Sartre's adopted daughter Arlette Elkaïm-Sartre. Some of their discussions appear in Jean-Paul Sartre and Benny Lévy, *Hope Now: The 1980 Interviews*, trans. Adrian van den Houven (Chicago: University of Chicago Press, 1996). More generally on Sartre's refusal to collude with antisemitism, see Jonathan Judaken, *Jean-Paul Sartre and The Jewish Question: Anti-Antisemitism and the Politics of the French Intellectual* (Lincoln: University of Nebraska Press, 2006).

53 This alarming episode is discussed in some detail in Hans Kundnani, *Utopia or Auschwitz: Germany's 1968 Generation and the Holocaust* (New York: Columbia University Press, 2009), 88–91. On the reluctance of the radical left to address the antisemitism revealed by this incident, see the interview with Tilman Fichter, the brother of one of those who planted the bomb: 'The Antisemitism of the 68ers' in *signandsight: Let's Talk European*, 31 October 2005, www.signandsight.com/features/434.html (accessed 4 December 2015).

54 Ernest Mandel (1999) 'Prémisses Matérielles, Sociales et Idéologiques du Génocide Nazi' in Gilbert Achcar (ed.), *Le Marxisme d'Ernest Mandel* (Paris: Presses Univer-sitaires de France, 1999), 200–202.

55 On relations between imperialism and genocide, see amongst others the pioneering work of Dirk Moses, *Empire, Colony, Genocide: Conquest, Occupation, and Subaltern Resistance in World History* (Oxford: Berghahn, 2008); Donald Bloxham, *The Final Solution: A Genocide* (Oxford: Oxford University Press, 2009); and Dan Stone, *Histories of the Holocaust* (Oxford: Oxford University Press, 2010), especially ch. 5 on 'Genocide, the Holocaust and the History of Colonialism'. On Nazi empire-building in the East, see Wendy Lower, *Nazi Empire-Building and the Holocaust* (University of North Carolina Press: Chapel Hill, 2007); Mark Mazower, *Hitler's Empire: How the Nazis Ruled Europe* (New York: Penguin Press, 2008). For a more detailed discussion of these issues, see Philip Spencer, 'Imperialism, Anti-Imperialism and the Problem of Genocide, Past and Present', *History*, 98, October 2013: 606–622.

56 There were significant differences as well as similarities between the ways in which the Nazis conceived of the Jews and other victims of imperialist racism, a difference captured well by Enzo Traverso: 'In contrast to the imperialist view of the colonised, Nazism did not regard the Jews as a backward, savage, primitive people or one that was incapable of surviving the onward march of progress. It considered them not as an archaic element that had lingered on the path of civilisation but as civilisation's enemy'. Enzo Traverso, *The Origins of Nazi Violence* (New York: New Press, 2003), 74.

57 The downplaying of the Jewish aspect of oppression by Communist intellectuals is very well caught in a memoir of a daughter's relation to her Hungarian Jewish Communist father. See Yudit Kiss, *The Summer My Father Died* (London: Telegram Books, 2012).

58 Max Horkheimer, 'The Jews and Europe' in Stephen Eric Bronner and Douglas Kellner (eds.), *Critical Theory and Society* (London: Routledge, 1989 [1938]), 77–94.

59 Horkheimer, 'The Jews and Europe', 89.

60 Rolf Wiggershaus, *The Frankfurt School: Its History, Theories, and Political Significance* (Cambridge: Polity Press, 1994), 364.

61 Horkheimer, 'The Jews and Europe', 92.

62 Franz Neumann, *Behemoth: The Structure and Practice of National Socialism* (London: Frank Cass, 1967), 125. Detlev Claussen argues that the 'inner circle' of the Frankfurt School did not accept Neumann's analysis when it was presented. Detlev Claussen, *Grenzen der Aufklarung: zur Gesellschaflichen Geschichte der Modernen Antisemitismus* (Frankfurt am Main: Fischer, 1987), 46.

63 Neumann, *Behemoth*, 125; 551; 221; 467.

64 Quoted in Anson Rabinbach, 'The Cunning of Unreason: Mimesis and the Construction of Antisemitism in Horkheimer and Adorno's *Dialectic of Enlightenment*' in *In the Shadow of Catastrophe: German Intellectuals Between Apocalypse and Enlightenment*, Berkeley: University of California Press, 2001), 184.

65 Some of the work of members of the Frankfurt School for the US government has now been published in Franz Neumann, Herbert Marcuse and Otto Kirchheimer, *Secret Reports on Nazi Germany: The Frankfurt School Contribution to the War Effort*, ed. Raffaelle Laudani (Princeton, N.J.: Princeton University Press 2013).

66 For a broader discussion of this question, see Jacob Katz, 'Was the Holocaust Predictable?' in Yehuda Bauer and Nathan Rotenstreich (eds.), *The Holocaust as Historical Experience* (New York: Holmes and Meier, 1981), 23–41.

67 Frank Chalk and Kurt Jonassen, *The History and Sociology of Genocide* (New Haven: Yale University Press, 1990), 324.

68 Detlev Claussen, *Adorno: The Last Genius* (Cambridge, MA.: Belknap Press of Harvard University Press, 2008), 235.

69 Claussen, *Adorno*, 235.

70 Max Horkheimer, *Gesammelte Schriften vol. 16 Briefwechsel 1937–40*, ed. Gunzelin Schmid Noerr (Frankfurt am Main: Fischer, 1995), 764.

71 Letter from Adorno to Horkheimer 2 October 1941, quoted in Wiggershaus, *The Frankfurt School*, 309.

72 Max Horkheimer, *Gesammelte Schriften vol. 17 Briefwechsel 1941–48*, ed. Gunzelin Schmid Noerr (Frankfurt am Main: Fischer, 1996), 599.

73 Horkheimer, *Gesammelte Schriften vol. 17*, 463–464.

74 James Schmidt, 'Genocide and the Limits of Enlightenment: Horkheimer and Adorno Revisited' in James Kaye and Bo Strath (eds.), *Enlightenment and Genocide: Contradictions of Modernity* (Brussels: Peter Lang, 2000), 81–102.

75 Max Horkheimer and Theodor W. Adorno, 'Research Project on Anti-Semitism', *Studies in Philosophy and Social Science*, 9 (1), 1941: 124–143.

76 See Eva Maria Ziege, *Antisemitismus und Gesellschaftstheorie: Die Frankfurter Schule im Amerikanischen Exil* (Berlin: Suhrkamp 2009); Thomas Wheatland, *The Frankfurt School in Exile* (Minneapolis; University of Minnesota Press, 2009).

77 Max Horkheimer and Theodor. W. Adorno, *Dialectic of Enlightenment* (London: Allen Lane, 1973 [1943]).

78 Rosa Luxemburg, 'The Junius Pamphlet: The Crisis in German Social Democracy' in *Rosa Luxemburg Speaks* ed. Mary-Alice Waters (New York: Pathfinder, 1970), 269.

79 Taner Akcam, A Shameful Act: The Armenian Genocide and the Question of Turkish Responsibility (London: Constable 2007), xvi.

80 Omer Bartov, 'Extreme Violence and the Scholarly Community', *International Social Science Journal*, 54 (174), 2002: 509–518, at 510. On connections between the genocides of the Herero and Nama and that of the Jews, see Jürgen Zimmerer 'The Birth of the *Ostland* out of the Spirit of Colonialism: A Postcolonial Perspective on the Nazi Policy of Conquest and Extermination', *Patterns of Prejudice* 39 (2), 2005: 197–219; and Benjamin Madley, 'From Africa to Auschwitz: How German South West Africa Incubated Ideas and Methods Adopted and Developed by the Nazis in Eastern Europe', *European History Quarterly*, 35, 2005: 429–464. For a more sceptical view, which lays stress on developments inside Germany, see Robert Gerwarth and Stephan Malinowksi, 'Hannah Arendt's Ghosts: Reflections on the Disputable Path from Windhoek to Auschwitz', *Central European History*, 42, 2009: 279–300, and from an angle that emphasises the role of German military traditions, Isabel Hull *Absolute Destruction: Military Culture and the Practices of War in Imperial Germany* (Ithaca, N.Y.: Cornell University Press, 2005).

81 Klaus-Michael Mallmann and Martin Cüppers, *Nazi Palestine: The Plans for the Extermination of the Jews of Palestine* (New York: Enigma Books with United States Holocaust Museum, 2010).

82 See Martin Jay, 'The Jews and the Frankfurt School: Critical Theory's Analysis of Anti-Semitism' in Jack Zipes and Anson Rabinbach (eds.), *Germans and Jews Since the Holocaust* (New York: Holmes and Meier, 1986), 293.

83 Anson Rabinbach, 'Why Were the Jews Sacrificed? The Place of Antisemitism in *Dialectic of Enlightenment*', *New German Critique* 81, 2000: 49–64, at 61.

84 Horkheimer and Adorno, *Dialectic of Enlightenment*, 176.

85 Horkheimer and Adorno. *Dialectic of Enlightenment*, 168.

86 Horkheimer and Adorno, *Dialectic of Enlightenment*, 169.

87 Horkheimer and Adorno, *Dialectic of Enlightenment*, 170.

88 Horkheimer and Adorno, *Dialectic of Enlightenment*, 170.

89 Horkheimer and Adorno, *Dialectic of Enlightenment*, 170–171.

90 Horkheimer and Adorno, *Dialectic of Enlightenment*, 173, 174.

91 Horkheimer and Adorno, *Dialectic of Enlightenment*, 175.

92 Horkheimer and Adorno, *Dialectic of Enlightenment*, 176.

93 Horkheimer and Adorno, *Dialectic of Enlightenment*, 177.

94 Horkheimer and Adorno, *Dialectic of Enlightenment*, 179.

95 Horkheimer and Adorno, *Dialectic of Enlightenment*, 183.

96 Horkheimer and Adorno, *Dialectic of Enlightenment*, 176. David Nirenberg puts it well: 'what gave anti-Semitic ideas their power was not so much their relation to reality, but rather their exemption from reality checks – that is from the critical testing to which so many other concepts were subjected'. Nirenberg, *Anti-Judaism*, 466.

97 Horkheimer and Adorno, *Dialectic of Enlightenment*, 187.

98 Horkheimer and Adorno, *Dialectic of Enlightenment*, 189–190.

99 Horkheimer and Adorno, *Dialectic of Enlightenment*, 186.

100 Horkheimer and Adorno, *Dialectic of Enlightenment*, 193.
101 Horkheimer and Adorno, *Dialectic of Enlightenment*, 187.
102 Horkheimer and Adorno, *Dialectic of Enlightenment*, 196–197.
103 Horkheimer and Adorno, *Dialectic of Enlightenment*, 191.
104 Horkheimer and Adorno, *Dialectic of Enlightenment*, 197.
105 Horkheimer and Adorno, *Dialectic of Enlightenment*, 199.
106 Horkheimer and Adorno, *Dialectic of Enlightenment*, 192.
107 Horkheimer and Adorno, *Dialectic of Enlightenment*, 186.
108 Horkheimer and Adorno, *Dialectic of Enlightenment*, 193.
109 Horkheimer and Adorno, *Dialectic of Enlightenment*, 186.
110 Theodor W. Adorno, *Guilt and Defense: On the Legacies of National Socialism in Postwar Germany*, ed. Jeffrey K. Olick and Andrew J. Perrin (Cambridge, MA: Harvard University Press 2010).
111 Claussen argues that antisemitism was the key issue that led Adorno and Horkheimer to break with the student movement. Claussen, *Grenzen der Aufklarung*, 14.
112 Walter Benjamin has famously insisted that history needs to be considered from the vantage point of those whose lives are wrecked, even to the point of almost complete destruction. Benjamin, 'Theses on the Philosophy of History'. On the connection between Benjamin's general perspective here and Horkheimer and Adorno's specific approach to the Holocaust (much of which Benjamin did not live to see since he died trying to flee the Nazis in 1940 before the extermination project began in earnest), see Orietta Ombrosi, *The Twilight of Reason: W. Benjamin, T.W. Adorno, M. Horkheimer and E. Levinas, tested by the Catastrophe* (Boston, MA: Academic Studies Press, 2012).
113 On the need for and impediment to reflection and self-reflection, see Claussen, *Grenzen der Aufklarung*, 14 ff.
114 Horkheimer and Adorno, *Dialectic of Enlightenment*, 199–200.

4

Political life in an antisemitic world: Hannah Arendt's Jewish writings

> All I wanted was to be a man among other men. I wanted to come lithe and young into a world that was ours and to help to build it together. (Franz Fanon, *The Fact of Blackness*)[1]

> We can never become just Netherlanders, or just English or representatives of any country for that matter. We will always remain Jews, but we want to, too. (Anne Frank, *The Diary of a Young Girl*)[2]

At the time that Horkheimer and Adorno were rethinking their approach to modern antisemitism, Hannah Arendt was also embarking on her own sustained efforts to understand the phenomenon. Initially, she had shown little interest in the question of antisemitism, which she professed had previously 'bored' her, but with the rise of Hitler, antisemitism unsurprisingly became a key concern of hers both politically and intellectually.[3] Arendt was active in Zionist movements, initially in Germany and then in France after she took refuge there in 1933. In the nation state that had proclaimed the Rights of Man and Citizen and accorded citizenship rights to Jews, she found herself extremely vulnerable as a stateless person. After the Nazis swept through France, Arendt was interned, escaped and made her way to the United States where, like Horkheimer and Adorno, she sought to come to terms with something which, in her mind, fundamentally altered the conditions not only of Jewish life but also of human existence.

Modernity and antisemitism

In an interview conducted in 1964, Arendt reflected on the impact that news of Auschwitz had on her in terms that echo Adorno and Horkheimer's rethinking at the time.

> What was decisive for me was not the year 1933 ... What was decisive was the day we learned about Auschwitz ... in 1943 ... At first we didn't believe

it ... because militarily it was unnecessary and uncalled for. Before that, we said, well one has enemies. That is natural. Why shouldn't people have enemies? But this was different. It was as if an abyss had opened up. We had the idea that amends could be made for everything else. Amends can be made for almost anything at some point in politics. But not for this. This ought never to have happened ... Something happened there to which we cannot reconcile ourselves.[4]

Like Horkheimer and Adorno, Arendt also argued that there is something about modern antisemitism that radically distinguishes it from earlier forms of anti-Judaic prejudice. Jews may always have had enemies but this was of a different order. She understood antisemitism as a modern phenomenon of ancient vintage. Its earlier elements did not necessarily disappear but they were rearticulated in the modern age:

> It goes without saying that modern antisemitism is the heir to medieval antecedents and thus to the ancient hatred of Jews as well ... there are scarcely any medieval accusations, from ritual murder to usury, that cannot be found verbatim in some modern piece of filthy literary trash.[5]

In emphasising the *modernity* of antisemitism, Arendt wanted to show that it is a phenomenon of shorter durée than anti-Judaism but of longer durée than those who position it always in the past. Antisemitism has deep roots in modern society even though modern society also has its own critical resources with which to combat it. While it is mistaken to naturalise antisemitism as a permanent property of relations between Jews and non-Jews, there are periods and places in which it appears obsolete, a zombie-concept in the language of cosmopolitanism, only to re-emerge in surprising new forms.[6] Modern antisemitism has long historical antecedents, but what was more urgent than reviewing its pre-history was to think about why Jews were once again defined as a 'question' in modern times and how this was tied up with the concerns of those who put this 'question'.[7] The emphasis on the *modernity* of antisemitism is something most exponents of critical theory have in common but the specific aim of Arendt's discussion was not to relegate antisemitism to the past, as may be the case if we see ourselves now living in a post-modern condition, but on the contrary to reveal the possibility of ongoing transmutations.[8]

As we have seen, Arendt held that although the Jewish question was posed in the Enlightenment in quite different ways and for quite different ends than it was by antisemites, in support of Jewish emancipation rather than against it, the Enlightenment provided 'classic antisemitism its theoretical basis'.[9] She argued that what distinguished modern secular antisemitism from medieval religious

hatred of Jews, was a legacy of Enlightenment: it was the abstraction of 'the Jew'
as a principle of evil:

> Modern antisemitism, which knows that Jews are not universally 'noxious', turns
> this abstraction on its head by overlooking the existence of 'decent' Jews with
> whom one may be personally acquainted ('there are decent Jews everywhere') in
> favour of *the* Jew, who has at last been discovered to be the evil principle of history
> ... To transform the Jew from a living individual into a principle, into an agglom-
> eration of characteristics that are universally 'evil' and, although observable in other
> people as well, are always called 'Jewish' (whereas any others have been 'Judaized'),
> in short to transform the Jew into *the* Jew and then to conjure up all the things
> that are *Jewish* about him – all of these are tendencies found throughout modern
> antisemitism, which in its essence can be distinguished from the medieval hatred
> of Jews precisely because of its abstractness.[10]

Within the terms of the Jewish question 'the Jew' was defined as the other of
the universal, whether the universal was equated with nations, states, the race,
the international or indeed humanity. Arendt wrote in this vein:

> Since the Jew no longer has an indisputable identity in Western European nations,
> one of the antisemite's most urgent needs is to define him. Whether the Jews are
> a religion or a nation, a people or a race, a state or a tribe, depends on the specific
> opinion non-Jews – in whose midst Jews live – have about themselves, but it
> certainly has no connection whatever with any germinal knowledge about the Jews.
> As the peoples of Europe became nations, the Jews became a 'nation within the
> nation'; as the Germans began to see in the state something more than their
> political representation, that is, as their fundamental 'essence', the Jews became a
> state within a state. As the word 'international' began to bounce around inside
> people's heads, Jews came to represent the 'international of gold', and a bit later,
> by an ingenious combination of state and international, to advance – in the form
> of the 'elders of Zion' – to an international state. And ... when the Germans
> transformed themselves at last into Aryans, we have been wandering through world
> history as Semites, just as it is to the arrogance of the Anglo-Saxon 'white man'
> over against colonial peoples that we owe the epithet 'white nigger'.[11]

It was paradoxically the universalism of the modern age that set the terms for
the rise of modern antisemitism.

On the responsibility of victims

Like Adorno and Horkheimer, Arendt understood that the negative projections
imposed on 'the Jew' had to do with the phantasies of those who made these
projections rather than with the actual behaviour or characteristics of Jews
themselves. This is not to say, however, that antisemitism in its own distorted

and distorting ways did not have some connection with the realities of Jewish life. Arendt observed that nineteenth-century antisemitism – with its tales of conspiracy, money and parasitism and its references to 'a secret world power which makes and unmakes governments', a 'secret force behind the throne', a power that holds Europe 'in its thrall' – exploited transient and partial historical moments of Jewish history to convert them into the fictitious expression of a noxious Jewish essence. Some antisemitic stereotypes were constructed out of the history of 'Court Jews' who, with inter-European networks at their disposal, played a significant role in financing European monarchs in the seventeenth and eighteenth centuries, and who evolved into international banking houses when nineteenth-century European states extended this system of privileges to meet their own expanding financial needs. The history of every category of people contains 'misdeeds' among some of its members that serve as fuel for the racist imagination, though the racist imagination is not limited to any such real or imagined misdeeds, and this was true of the Jews as well. Arendt saw that when the system of state privileges broke down in the latter half of the nineteenth century, when Jewish financiers lost their hegemonic role in state transactions and were replaced by national entrepreneurs attracted by the profits to be won through colonial conquest, antisemitism did not disappear but became more remote from social reality – the preserve of 'charlatans and crackpots' with their 'weird admixture of half-truths and wild superstitions'.[12] Arendt showed that after the First World War, antisemitism 'emancipated itself from all specific Jewish deeds and misdeeds' and became 'severed from all actual experience concerning the Jewish people'.[13] In genocidal antisemitism there arose an obverse relation between the actual situation of Jews, who were 'cruelly powerless', and the 'fables of monstrous, diabolic and secret power' constructed by Nazis.[14] Arendt concluded that in all its forms, those that still had some connection with reality and those which lost all connection, 'the foundations of antisemitism are found in developments that have very little to do with Jews'.[15]

It is worth stressing this point since Arendt has been read as attributing responsibility or at least co-responsibility to Jews for the rise of antisemitism.[16] In *The Origins of Totalitarianism* she criticised theories of antisemitism that deny 'all specific Jewish responsibility' for its emergence and held that the origins of antisemitism 'must be found in certain aspects of Jewish history and specifically Jewish functions during the last centuries'.[17] Arendt's emphasis on Jewish responsibility exposed her to the criticism that she focused on the *transgressions* of Jews – they 'avoided all political action for two thousand years';[18] rich Jews involved themselves in 'shady transactions';[19] Jewish finance manipulated 'the business of the state',[20] etc. – and postulated an excessively 'intimate relationship' between antisemitic phantasies and the realities of Jewish life. She seemed to share an assumption, which as we have seen was common within the German left, that there was some truth to antisemitic images of Jews.[21] She even seemed to rely at times on antisemitic sources to illustrate what Jews were really like. Two cases in point were her citation of an opponent of Jewish emancipation, Heinrich Paulus (1761–1851), and of a National Socialist historian, Walter Frank (1905–1945), to back up claims that Jews were inclined toward 'national isolation' or that 'rich Jews' curried political favour with undemocratic states at the expense of the 'Jewish masses'.[22] What has most perturbed some critics is Arendt's claim that these sources could be 'consulted with profit' to find out anything worthwhile about the realities of Jewish life.[23]

Some recent readers of Arendt have written approvingly of her co-responsibility thesis in the following sense, that they hold the behaviour of the Jewish state or the ideology of Jewish nationalism or the worldwide machinations of Zionism responsible or partly responsible for outbreaks of antisemitism in the current period.[24] In our view, however, we should no more accept the contention that there was a specific Jewish co-responsibility for the rise of antisemitism than we should accept the argument that black people are co-responsible for racism, women co-responsible for sexism, or Muslims co-responsible for Islamophobia. While Arendt wanted to restore some sense of Jewish agency, and not merely victimhood, in her analysis of antisemitism, this cannot justify the co-responsibility argument. To address Arendt's contribution to our understanding of responsibility, we need to make a distinction she did not always observe: between how Jews have *responded* to antisemitism and their *responsibility for* antisemitism. In the use of language Arendt strayed over this line, but her considered judgment was summed up in the statement that to treat the behaviour of Jews as the source of antisemitism is 'the malicious and stupid insight of antisemites, who think that this vile tenet can account for hecatombs of human sacrifice'.[25] Arendt may not have been wholly consistent, but at the core of her argument lay a refusal on the one hand to blame the Jews for antisemitism and on the other to rationalise Jewish responses to antisemitism.

If the response of victims is consequential, if it affects outcomes, then it becomes a matter of concern how Jewish responses to antisemitism were forged and whether they closed off or opened up the potential for solidarity from other people. For it is in the nature of genocide that the targeted group alone rarely has the resources to defend itself against the power of perpetrators equipped with a monopoly of the means of coercion and backed by popular mobilisation. In the Holocaust Jews, largely defenceless, could not by themselves defeat the forces of antisemitism, and their search for solidarity puts an urgent slant on Arendt's question of whether the 'final solution' was understood 'only' as a crime against the Jewish people, an extreme episode in 'the long history of Jew-hatred and anti-Semitism', or as a crime against humanity, an attack on human diversity as such.[26] One of Arendt's main concerns in her report on the Eichmann trial in 1963 was the prosecution's failure to understand that in the 'final solution' humankind in its entirety was 'grievously hurt and endangered'. It reinforced the very problem that the category of 'crimes against humanity' was intended to address: the breaking up of the human race into a multitude of competing nations, each pursuing its own interests, each fighting its own battles, each uninterested in the fate of others. Arendt wanted to show that the universal and particular aspects of the genocide were inseparable, or as she put it, that the 'final solution' was a 'crime against humanity ... perpetrated on the body of the Jewish people'.[27]

The issue of responsibility Arendt raised was how victims responded to the *dual* aspect of the threat they faced – as Jews and as human beings. She maintained that the two types of political consciousness she addressed, assimilationism and Zionism, were both one-sided: assimilationism identifies with the 'universal' at the expense of the 'particular', which it treats as a defect, while Zionism identifies with the 'particular' at the expense of the 'universal', which it treats as an illusion and a trap. Arendt was critical of Jewish assimilationism for looking away from antisemitism altogether and of Zionism for confronting antisemitism exclusively from a national point of view. The alternative Arendt reached out for was that of a cosmopolitan form of solidarity that can reconcile the universal and the particular in the struggle against antisemitism, but this proved to be an elusive prize. She could not accept an abstract cosmopolitanism that deluded itself into thinking that it could rise above all particular concerns. Assimilationism, Zionism and cosmopolitanism all provided an occasion for antisemitic stereotypes denigrating respectively the 'parvenu Jew', the 'Zionist Jew' and the 'rootless cosmopolitan Jew'. Arendt, however, did not explore these types of political consciousness through the suspicious eyes of the antisemite but through the experience of Jews confronted with the difficulties of finding a home in a world poisoned by antisemitism.

On assimilationist responses to antisemitism

Arendt observed that a great temptation facing Jews who sought absorption into national societies brimming with anti-Jewish prejudice was to regard everything *particular* about themselves as Jews as 'an impediment to ... their becoming full human beings'.[28] In her study of *Rahel Varnhagen* (written in the 1930s and first published in 1958) Arendt put the issue thus: 'In a society on the whole hostile to the Jews – and that situation obtained in all countries in which Jews lived, down to the twentieth century – it is possible to assimilate only by assimilating to anti-Semitism also'.[29] In *The Origins of Totalitarianism* (first published in 1951 and mainly written in the 1940s) Arendt maintained that 'all advocates of emancipation called for assimilation as either a preliminary condition to Jewish emancipation or its automatic consequence'. She commented, albeit with more passion than empirical evidence, that the vast majority of Jews in Germany and Austria became indifferent to or complicit with the upsurge of antisemitism that accompanied their emancipation.

Faced with the growth of modern political antisemitism – and more broadly of a sense of the inherent difference of 'the Jews' as an alien category of people – the tried-and-tested assimilationist response seemed to Arendt self-defeating. It called for the redoubling of efforts to assimilate into increasingly antisemitic societies through 'slavish' expressions of exaggerated patriotism, gratitude and trust in 'whatever government happened to be in power' without noticing how untrustworthy this made Jews appear in the eyes of every successive government.[30]

Arendt argued that assimilationists could never get to grips with the modernity of antisemitism. They presented it as an outmoded prejudice inexorably coming to an end in the modern era, and simply closed their eyes to the evolution of new forms of antisemitism.[31] In spite of Sisyphean efforts to integrate into antisemitic societies, assimilationists were 'never able to explain how things could ever have turned out so badly'.[32] They reduced the otherness of Jews to a 'harmless difference of religion' and, in a manner reminiscent of von Dohm, attributed all further differences to old political conditions, which had 'corrupted the Jews by treating them badly'.[33] The poverty of assimilationism for Arendt lay in its reluctance to think about antisemitism at all. As she put it: 'one of the hallmarks of the Jewish world's response to the Jewish question is a total lack of interest in dealing with antisemitism'.[34]

Arendt explained the predominance of assimilationism in terms of the changing character of Jewish society. As antisemitic movements evolved in Europe, modern conditions were also gnawing away at the cohesion of Jewish communities, traditionally constructed around religious values and the protective role of Jewish notables. The result was that attacks on Jews from without met with loss of solidarity from within; not least, the exaggerated patriotism of assimilationist Jews was aligned to disdainful hostility to *Ostjuden*, Jewish migrants from the East. Some Jews imagined that political antisemitism might be not so bad since it at least kept the Jewish people intact just as Christian hostility to Jews once had. Some looked for local protection in the time-honoured but no longer effective ways of appealing to 'connections' wealthy Jews had with those in power. Some denied there was any significant antisemitism in society, declaring, for example, that Dreyfus just happened to be a Jew and that his persecution had nothing to do with his Jewishness. Assimilated Jews became less interested in Judaism than in their natural-born Jewishness, that is, the sense of Jewish origins without religious or ethical connotation which Marcel Proust called 'dejudaized Judaism'.[35] One of the threads of Arendt's argument was that the construction of 'Jewishness' among assimilated Jews dovetailed with antisemitic ways of thinking, inasmuch as Judaism no longer served as a faith that could be renounced but Jewishness served as the unchangeable core of one's being. While Jews were able to escape from Judaism, there was no escape from Jewishness.

A ferociously anti-bourgeois conviction drove Arendt's critique of assimilationism. She echoed the words of the French socialist Bernard Lazare (1865–1903), that assimilationism was a 'spurious doctrine' that would have Jews 'abandon all their characteristics, individual and moral alike' and enter into a 'double slavery … not only the wealthy of my people, who exploit and sell me, but also the rich and poor of other peoples who oppress and torture me in the name of my rich'.[36] Arendt commented that Jews who profited from this 'double slavery' were destined to 'pay the price of the whole wretched system' and be abandoned by those who used them as 'lackeys and henchmen'. She paid homage to the 'pariah politics' of 'those bold spirits who tried to make of the emancipation of the Jews that which it really should have been – an admission of Jews as *Jews* to the ranks of humanity, rather than a permit to ape the gentiles or an opportunity to play the parvenu'.[37] Arendt contrasted assimilationism to the 'bold spirit' of the pariah:[38] the 'conscious pariah', as Bernard Lazare put it, who proclaimed it 'the duty of every human being to resist oppression' of all human beings, as well as less overtly political types like Heinrich Heine's 'schlemiel', Charlie Chaplin's 'suspect' or Franz Kafka's 'man of good will'. What they had in common was 'practical experience of just how ambiguous is the freedom which emancipation has ensured … how treacherous the promise of equality which assimilation has held out'.[39] None, according to Arendt, was fooled by the illusion that 'by achieving emancipation the Jewish people had achieved a genuine freedom'. It was an illusion that ignored 'the condition which had characterised emancipation everywhere in Europe … that the Jew might only become a man when he ceased to be a Jew'.[40]

Now, Arendt's account of assimilationism has rightly been criticised for constructing a pejorative view of assimilated German Jews.[41] There is now a substantial literature describing the *various* creative paths of assimilation taken by Jews in Germany and elsewhere, which reveals a more complex picture of assimilated Jews than Arendt provided.[42] Not all were as complacent or as passive as she seems to suggest. Some did not conform to existing society, or rebelled against it in the name of its unachieved ideals. Some were politically engaged as liberals and socialists. Some did not place much value on their Jewish identity and saw themselves only as good liberals or good socialists. Some created new hybrid identities out of the encounter between Germans and Jews. And some, including Arendt herself, refused to discard their particularity as Jews in order to be accepted as universal human beings.

If we are to recover the force of Arendt's argument, we have more work to do. We need to make a distinction Arendt generally did not observe: that between assimilation and assimilationism. Arendt tended to use these concepts interchangeably but it makes little sense to treat Arendt as hostile to assimilation as such. She was, after all, a thoroughly assimilated German–Jewish intellectual. Her critique is undoubtedly reductive when aimed at assimilation as such, but it makes good sense when aimed at *assimilationism*, that is to say, a response to antisemitism that turns assimilation into the *raison d'être* of one's being in the world. While assimilation refers to processes of adjustment to prevailing social norms, which can take all manner of more or less creative forms, assimilationism prizes assimilation over all other values. Arendt is not to be blamed for facing up to the contradictions of assimilationism, that is to say, of a subjectivity that does everything it can to refute the existence of antisemitism, to put acceptance in society before solidarity with fellow Jews, and to represent oneself as an 'exception' to the Jewish norm. Assimilationism was a form of life of assimilated Jewish metropolitan intellectuals willing to come to terms with an ever more antisemitic society.[43]

On Zionist responses to antisemitism

The main political alternative to assimilationism Arendt addressed, and with which she had a deeply troubled relation, was that of Jewish nationalism and especially Zionism. Arendt was critical of Zionism but she worked with it and saw it as a *radical* response to the *failure* of assimilationists to face up to the attacks mounted by antisemites. In her 1964 interview with Gunther Gaus, she recollected her feeling that 'there was no alternative' and that 'it would have been pointless to work with the assimilated'.[44] In 1938 she wrote that she valued nationalist histories written from a Zionist perspective more than 'apologetic' histories written from an assimilationist perspective, since Zionists at least attempted to 'defend the honour of the Jewish people' and 'unify a scattered nation'.[45] She saw it as the strength of Zionism to recognise the existence of modern European antisemitism in a way that assimilationists were never able to do; but its weakness as she saw it was to naturalise antisemitism – to conceive the history of the Jews as one 'monotonous chronicle of persecution and mis-fortune', to put the notion of 'an eternal struggle of substances foreign to one another' before any social or historical relations, to treat hatred of Jews as a 'generalised fixation' that erased any distinction between friends and foes, to treat antisemitism as a relation between non-Jews and Jews that could be escaped but not changed.[46]Arendt saw Zionism as a response to persecution based on the credo that 'You can only defend yourself as the person you are attacked as. A person attacked as a Jew cannot defend himself as an Englishman or a French-man. The world would only conclude that he is simply not defending himself'.[47] Nonetheless she did not simply endorse this form of response. Zionism, like other nationalisms, offered a limited form of solidarity.

Arendt's analysis of Zionism was tied to the experience of other post-imperial nationalist movements, which accompanied the break-up of the multi-national empires (Ottoman, Russian, Austro-Hungarian, Prussian) that had dominated Europe and Asia until the First World War. They all based themselves on the conviction that 'emancipation could be attained only with national self-determination' and aimed to secure their 'own' nation states, at a time when there was a widespread consensus across the political spectrum that nations had a right to self-determination. Woodrow Wilson, President of the United States, and Lenin, leader of the Bolshevik Revolution, were opposed in almost every other respect, but converged over the existence of this right.[48] Arendt did not disagree but she drew attention to the reshaping of the political landscape on which this right was premised. While in its republican form the state had defined the nation in terms of common citizenship in a bounded political community, post-imperial nationalist movements reversed this relation. It was now the nation that defined the state and established internal divisions between those deemed to belong to the nation and those deemed to fall outside. Arendt wrote of the construction in newly independent states of a fourfold hierarchy: state-peoples who had a recognised claim to their own state; peoples said to be formally equal but unequal in fact; minorities sometimes legally recognised in international treaties; and stateless persons deprived of work, home, country and, as she famously put it, of the very 'right to have rights'.[49]

The danger Arendt discerned in Zionism was that the same kind of exclusionary nationalism which spread over the European continent in the interwar years was again rising to the surface in the Middle East. In an essay on *The Crisis of Zionism* (1943), she argued that 'the foundations of Zionism were laid during a time when nobody could imagine any other solution to minority or nationality problems than the autonomous national state with a homogeneous population'.[50] At the same time, and this was a crucial qualification, she warned against allowing a selective distrust of nationalism to be turned into a pretext for abandoning the project for a Jewish homeland. She looked for other solutions, including the idea of a federal state based on equal rights for all peoples following a model she saw *in nuce* in the United States, Soviet Union and Europe, but she never doubted the need to provide a safe place for those facing annihilation.

In *Zionism Reconsidered* (1944), Arendt argued that Zionism was the child not only of romantic nationalism but also of socialism. She expressed her admiration of left Zionists in Hashomer Hatza'ir and Poale Zion for the social experiments they carried out but criticised their indifference to Arab–Jewish co-operation, failure to support Jews and Arabs who looked to co-operation, and acceptance of terror against Arab populations.[51] Arendt was worried by a tendency toward 'revisionist attitudes' in mainstream Zionism, that is, the tendency to accept antisemitism as a 'fact' of the non-Jewish world, to adopt an intransigent stance on the Jewish–Arab conflict in Palestine, and to prioritise alliances with imperial powers against relations with their neighbours. She admired the militancy of Zionism but not the 'self-centredness' that had little interest in fighting alongside other revolutionary forces in Europe.[52] Whenever the Zionist movement in Palestine faced a choice between asking for 'protection from an outside power against their neighbours' and coming to 'a working agreement with their neighbours', Arendt saw it as inclined to choose the former: 'only folly could dictate a policy which trusts a distant imperial power for protection, while alienating the good will of neighbours'.[53] The point for Arendt was that this type of 'revisionism' did nothing to combat the antisemitism that existed among Arabs as well as Europeans.

Arendt argued that what came in to being in Palestine was a world of mutual denunciation: 'Jewish determination to keep and possibly extend national sovereignty without consideration for Arab interests, and Arab determination to expel the Jewish "invaders" from Palestine without consideration for Jewish achievements there'.[54] The result was that a small national conflict in the Middle East, which bore a disturbing resemblance to that of small nations in Europe in the interwar period, was magnified and distorted in terms of 'sinister behind-the-scenes conspiracy'. Arabs saw themselves confronted by the forces of imperialism, Jews saw themselves confronted by two thousand years of antisemitic history; both treated their opponents not as a 'concrete human being' but as a kind of 'ghost' or 'phantom'.[55] Arendt saw it as a basic task of critical thought to exorcise these phantoms and foster a changed attitude among both Jews and Arabs: 'recognition of the existence of the state of Israel on one side and of the existence of an Arab population in Palestine and the Near East on the other'.[56]

To make sense of Arendt's critical stance, we need again to make a distinction she did not always observe: between the project of building a homeland in which Jews could find refuge, and that of constructing an exclusionary nation state. Arendt's appraisal of Zionism was founded on a distinction between the right of national self-determination and the political reversions and ideological mystifications generated by exclusive nationalism. Recognition of the right of peoples to collective self-determination at local, national and transnational levels is not at all the same thing as an ideology that turns the nation into the supreme source of political sovereignty. Her search was for new forms of territorial entity.

Equivocations of cosmopolitanism

So far we find in Arendt's Jewish writings a twofold critique: on one side, the critique of an assimilationism whose wilful blindness in the face of the gathering menace set the scene for its failure; on the other, the critique of a Zionism rendered normatively suspect by its naturalistic understanding of antisemitism. To do justice to Arendt's Jewish writings, we should keep both sides in mind.[57] We should also keep in mind that Arendt adopted a developmental approach to her analysis of Jewish consciousness in the face of modern antisemitism. She saw Zionism, for all its fault-lines, as an *advance* over assimilationism – as a response to antisemitism that was more political, more radical and more attractive to the Jewish masses than the assimilationism it opposed.

The Eichmann trial of 1960–1961 brought Arendt's critical relation to assimilationism and Zionism to the forefront of political debate. Arendt travelled to Jerusalem to attend some of the trial and published her 'report' at first in the New Yorker and then as the monograph *Eichmann in Jerusalem: A Report on the Banality of Evil.* The accused, Adolf Eichmann, had been in charge of the Nazi transportation of Jews to the death and labour camps. He escaped prosecution after the war, joined other Nazi escapees in Argentina, was seized by the Israeli secret services and put on trial in Israel. His trial provided a major opportunity, perhaps the first, to address the phenomenon of genocidal antisemitism in a public forum.[58] The trial also provided an occasion for Arendt to concretise her critique of Zionism and develop her own cosmopolitan leanings. Her assessment of the trial was equivocal. On the one hand, she had no problem with the abduction of Eichmann from Argentina, a country where there was little chance of extradition; no problem with an Israeli court prosecuting Eichmann for crimes committed almost entirely against Jews; no problem with the guilty verdict or the death penalty imposed on Eichmann. To the criticism that the trial ought to have been the work of an international criminal court, she defended the right of Israel to hold the trial and pointed out that in any event, there was no international criminal court. To the criticism that the trial might appear as a form of vengeance, she argued that it depended on how the trial was conducted.

On the other hand, Arendt criticised the prosecution, and in particular the prosecutor Gideon Hausner, for losing sight of the universalistic promise contained in the notion of 'crimes against humanity': she heard the voice of Jewish chauvinism in his privileging the new offence of 'crimes against the Jewish people' over that of 'crimes against humanity', in his failure to understand that humankind in its entirety had been 'grievously hurt and endangered' by the attack on Jews, in his appeals to Old Testament conceptions of vengeance over secular legality, and most controversially in his refusal to face up to the complicity of some members of the Jewish councils (*Judenräte* and *Jüdischen Ältestenräte*) in the execution of the 'final solution' – and that not all Jews were victims or heroes.[59]

For Arendt the 'final solution' – the terms *Shoah* and *Holocaust* were not yet used in this context – was not *only* to be understood in the context of the long history of antisemitism but *also* as an attack on the very idea of 'humanity'.[60] More than fifteen years earlier, in response to the Nuremberg trials, she had sought to expand the idea of guilt beyond national identity markers. She maintained in a cosmopolitan spirit that what was done to Jews raised questions not only of German guilt but also 'of what man is capable'. In an essay of 'universal responsibility' she wrote:

For many years now we have met Germans who declare that they are ashamed of being German, I have often felt tempted to answer that I am ashamed of being human ... For the idea of humanity ... has the very serious consequence that ... men must assume responsibility for all crimes committed by men and that all nations share the onus of evil committed by all others ... In political terms, the idea of humanity, excluding no people and assigning a monopoly of guilt to no one, is the only guarantee that one 'superior race' after another may not feel obligated to ... exterminate 'inferior races unworthy of survival' ... It becomes daily clearer how great a burden mankind is for man. Perhaps those Jews, to whose forefathers we owe the first conception of the idea of humanity, knew something about that burden when each year they used to say 'Our Father and King, we have sinned before you', taking not only the sins of their own community but all human offences upon themselves. Those who today are ready to follow this road in a modern version do not content themselves with the hypocritical confession 'God be thanked, I am not like that' ... Rather in fear and trembling have they finally realized of what man is capable – and this is indeed the precondition of modern political thinking ... only upon them, who are filled with a genuine fear of the inescapable guilt of the human race, can there be any reliance when it comes to fighting fearlessly, uncompromisingly, everywhere against the incalculable evil that men are capable of bringing about.[61]

Arendt had argued in 1945 for a universal conception of 'humanity': that human beings must assume responsibility for all the crimes committed by human beings and that a monopoly of guilt should be assigned to no one nation. She saw the idea of 'universal responsibility' as all that was left of the once noble idea of international solidarity. Now in the early 1960s she again picked up this cosmopolitan thread. What was most dramatically on display in the figure of Eichmann was the incapacity to imagine sharing a common world with Jews or see the world from their point of view. This was at once an attack both on Jews and on the idea of humanity itself.

the fate of the Jews has become today the symbol of what appears to be the rule of the devil on earth ... it is in the very nature of things human that every act that has once made its appearance and has been recorded in the history of mankind stays with mankind as potentiality ... if genocide is an actual possibility of the future, then no people on earth – least of all, of course, the Jewish people, in Israel or elsewhere – can feel reasonably sure of its continued existence.[62]

The trial of Eichmann re-raised the question of what it is to be human, for the project in which he participated was in effect an attempt to eradicate the very idea of the human status.[63] In *Mein Kampf* Hitler denounced universalism as a mode of Jewish domination designed to weaken the racial struggle. For Hitler it did not matter if universalism took the form of Christianity, liberalism, socialism or cosmopolitanism, for in all its guises it was the invention of the Jews in their ceaseless endeavour to seize power and profit.[64] The genocide of Jews was not just one for Jews to respond to but for everyone who wished to defend the idea of humanity against its assailants.

If we are right in saying that the main thread of Arendt's argument was a cosmopolitan thread, the fury with which her report on the trial was met within the Jewish political and intellectual community indicates how little it was understood. Her cosmopolitan leanings, defence of universalism and critique of Jewish chauvinism gave rise to the impression among some of her readers that she lacked human compassion and, more specifically, that she lacked compassion for the Jewish people. Gershom Scholem wrote to Arendt after the publication of her work objecting to the 'sneering' tone she used in speaking of her fellow Jews, focusing exclusively on 'the *weakness* of the Jewish stance in the world' and writing in a 'heartless ... and malicious tone' on matters that touched 'the very quick of our life'. Scholem accused Arendt of lacking love for the Jewish people, *Ahabath Israel* in Hebrew, which he described as typical of 'so many intellectuals who came from the German left'.[65] In response, Arendt re-affirmed her cosmopolitan leanings in a clever and honest way by attributing to Scholem's reprimand a quite different meaning:

> You are quite right – I am not moved by any 'love' of this sort, and for two reasons: I have never in my life 'loved' any people or collective – neither the German people, nor the French, nor the American, nor the working class, or anything of that sort. I indeed 'love' only my friends and the only kind of love I know of and believe in is the love of persons. Secondly, this 'love of the Jews' would appear to me, since I am Jewish myself, as something rather suspect. I cannot love myself or anything which I know is part and parcel of my own person ... The greatness of this people [the Jews] was once that it believed in God ... And now this people believes only in itself? What good can come out of that? – Well, in this sense I do not 'love' the Jews nor do I 'believe' in them; I merely belong to them as a matter of course, beyond dispute or argument.[66]

A cosmopolitan ethos infused Arendt's response to Scholem's condemnation. It looked on love for any nation with suspicion and love for one's own nation with special suspicion. Love is a personal and not a political matter; one has love for individuals and not for collectivities. The additional comment, that no good could come from a people who once believed in God now believing only in itself, echoed an observation she had made many years earlier in *The Origins of Totalitarianism*, that Judaism once meant 'the sharing of specific memories and specific hopes' but that in a secular age it tended to relapse into a 'simple fact of birth'.[67] In this context Arendt maintained that 'love for the Jewish people' could become a 'very real chauvinism ... a perverted nationalism in which (in the words of Chesterton) "the individual is himself the thing to be worshipped"'.[68]

Arendt's argument can best be understood if we distinguish between national-ism, i.e. making an 'ism' of the nation, and a simple sense of national belonging. In this case, her critique of Jewish nationalism was not at all incompatible with a strong sense of the rights of Jews, including the right of self-determination. She added a rider to the cosmopolitan tenor of her argument by acknowledging that 'wrong done *by* my own people naturally grieves me more than the wrong done by other peoples'. She maintained that she had always taken as given her mother's injunction that the wrongs done *to* her own people imposed on her, as a Jew, a particular responsibility to 'strike back'.[69] Arendt's twofold stance con-trasts both with those who attend *only* to the wrongs done *by* Jewish people and with those who attend *only* to the wrongs done *to* Jewish people. It gave genuine substance to her cosmopolitan ethos.

Our cosmopolitan existence

In her phenomenology of Jewish political consciousness, Arendt was critical of abstract forms of cosmopolitanism. She held that abstract cosmopolitanism could become merely a way of 'evading reality', the reality of who you are. She wrote of the 'pathos' of Jewish revolutionaries who preferred to 'play the revolu-tionary in the society of others but not in their own', and of Jewish intellectuals who imagined they could exist as 'pure human beings outside the range of peoples and nations'.[70] Regarding the phantasy that 'once the Jew was emanci-pated he would become more human, more free, and less prejudiced than other men', she described it as a 'gross expectation' lacking in elementary understand-ing.[71] In its abstract form of expression she likened cosmopolitanism to an international passport that gives you entry to every country in the world except your own.[72] For Arendt, cosmopolitanism was not to be conceived as a synthesis finally resolving the contradictions present in assimilationism and Zionism, but rather as itself a site of contradiction. In a Europe beset by genocidal antisemitism, the peril Arendt articulated was that cosmopolitanism could function as a facile denial of reality erasing the specificity of Jewish experience.[73] In her reply to Scholem, Arendt justifiably wrote that the 'Jewish problem ... has never been my problem'.[74] She was right about herself and alert to the danger of dressing up the 'Jewish problem' in a modern cosmopolitan garb.

Arendt's response to the abstraction of cosmopolitanism was similar to Marx's response to the abstraction of humanism: for Marx, it was not to reject human-ism but to construct a 'real humanism', as he put it; for Arendt, it was not to reject cosmopolitanism but to construct what we might call a 'real cosmopolitan-ism', which resisted turning the cosmopolitan ethos into an other-worldly ideal. Our 'cosmopolitan existence', she wrote in her *Lectures on Kant's Political Phi-losophy*, does not lie in dissociating ourselves from our particular identities and background but in nurturing the capacity to share a common world with others, to place oneself in the shoes of others, to see the world from the viewpoint of others. She wrote as follows:

> One judges always as a member of a community, guided by one's community sense, one's *sensus communis*. But in the last analysis, one is a member of a world community by the sheer fact of being human; this is one's 'cosmopolitan existence'. When one judges and when one acts in political matters, one is supposed to take one's bearing from the idea, not the actuality, of being a world citizen and therefore also a *Weltbetrachter*, a world spectator.[75]

'Common sense' refers to the experience of sharing of a common world with others; it requires the imagination to see the world from the standpoint of others. World citizenship and world spectatorship require what she called the 'enlarged mentality' capable of breaking free from the fetters of self-absorption. While they recognise the boundaries of one's communal grouping, they also push beyond these boundaries to behold the world through the eyes of the generalised other. It is a carefully crafted and balanced passage. Recognition of one's particular being as a member of this or that community is set against abstract cosmopolitanism; recognition of one's universal existence as a member of a world community is set against the allures of nationalism; recognition that judgment should be based on the *idea* of being a world citizen is set against the illusion that the world is actually cosmopolitan.

Arendt's idea of our 'cosmopolitan existence' incited the fury of some who were intent on defending Jewish chauvinism, and won the esteem of others who have used her work to legitimate antizionism. What both sets of commentators miss is Arendt's sense of the sheer modernity of the Jewish question and the oppressive weight of its legacy, which declares that Jews have to cease to be Jews in order to realise their humanity. The cosmopolitan existence to which Arendt referred is a struggle not only to overcome the prejudices of the so-called Jewish question, but also to recognise the inner strength of the three moments in the development of modern Jewish consciousness: the 'assimilated' moment of living one's life as a Jew in the diaspora, the 'Zionist' moment of living one's life as a citizen of Israel, and the 'cosmopolitan' moment of putting ourselves in the place of others, not least those for whose human suffering we bear some responsibility. There is no contradiction between these forms of life once we emancipate them from their respective 'isms' and cease to entrench them as hostile ways of being. What we wish to uncover in Arendt's Jewish writings is, we might say, a moderation wrought out of a deep and bold sense of rebellion against every absolute – be it old-fashioned assimilationism, a nationalistic Zionism, or even a cosmopolitan sense of moral superiority over those who identify with the Jewish nation.

For us this is the hallmark of Arendt's own striving for common sense and enlarged mentality.[76] It was haunted by recognition of the human condition of Jews after the Holocaust, which the return of the Jewish question was again threatening from within and without.

Notes

1 Franz Fanon, *The Fact of Blackness* [1952] in Les Back and John Solomos, trans Charles Markmann, *Theories of Race and Racism: A Reader* (London: Routledge, 2000), 259.

2 Anne Frank, *The Diary of a Young Girl*, 11 April, 1944, trans. B.M. Mooyaart (New York: Bantam, 1993).

3 Richard Bernstein, 'Hannah Arendt's Zionism' in Steven Aschheim (ed.), *Arendt in Jerusalem* (Berkeley: University of California Press 2001), 195.

4 Hannah Arendt 'What Remains? The Language Remains: A Conversation with Gunter Gaus' in Hannah Arendt, *Hannah Arendt: The Last Interview and Other Conversations* (Brooklyn, New York: Melville House 2013), 13–14.

5 Arendt, *Jewish Writings*, 65.

6 Regarding the aftermath of the Dreyfus affair, Arendt wrote: 'In *fin-de-siècle* society it was the antisemitism of the Dreyfus affair which opened society's doors to Jews … When the traitor was discovered to be the rather stupid victim of an ordinary frame-up … social interest in Jews subsided as quickly as did political antisemitism. Jews were again looked upon as ordinary mortals … When antisemitic legislation (later) forced society to oust the Jews … "admirers" of Jews finally became their murderers … It may be doubted that they were prominent among those who ran the death factories, although the percentage of the so-called educated classes among the actual killers is amazing. But it does explain the incredible disloyalty of precisely those strata of society that had known Jews most intimately'. Arendt, *Origins*, 86–87.

7 In *Anti-Judaism*, David Nirenberg situates antisemitism as a definite stage in the history of anti-Judaic thinking. He writes that it is 'a word that captures only a small portion, historically and conceptually' of what his book is about. Nirenberg also emphasises its lack of explanatory power: 'How and why do ideas about Jews and Judaism become convincing explanations for the state of the world? She [Arendt] rightly stressed the failure of "Antisemitism" as a sufficient explanation. The term *anti-Semite* effectively labels its targets as enemies of Jews and Judaism, but it does not do much to explain the nature of or reason for that enmity'. See Nirenberg, *Anti-Judaism*, 461–465.

8 Zygmunt Bauman offers one of the finest examples of sociological understanding of the modernity of antisemitism, but it is one that ultimately represents antisemitism as belonging to a now superseded age, the age of the first modernity as seen from the point of view of postmodernity. See Zygmunt Bauman, *Modernity and the Holocaust* (Cambridge: Polity, 1991) and *Modernity and Ambivalence* (Cambridge: Polity, 1993).

9 Arendt, *Jewish Writings*, 64.

10 Arendt, *Jewish Writings*, 64.

11 Arendt, *Jewish Writings*, 69.

12 Arendt, *Origins*, 53.

13 Arendt, *Origins*, 241, 229.

14 Arendt, *Jewish Writings*, 75.

15 Arendt, *Jewish Writings*, 75.

16 See the critiques of Arendt's approach to antisemitism in Peter Staudenmaier, 'Hannah Arendt's Analysis of Antisemitism in *The Origins of Totalitarianism*: A Critical Appraisal', *Patterns of Prejudice*, 46 (2), 2012: 154–179; and in Bernard Wasserstein in 'Blame the Victim: Hannah Arendt among the Nazis – The Historian and Her Sources', *Times Literary Supplement*, 9 October, 2009, 13–15. For a defence of Arendt against Wasserstein's charges see Irving Louis Horowitz, *Hannah Arendt, Radical Conservative* (New Jersey: Transaction Publishers, 2012), 1–12.

17 Arendt, *Origins*, 8–9.

18 Arendt, *Origins*, 8.

19 Arendt, *Origins*, 98.

20 Arendt, *Origins*, 99.

21 Arendt, *Origins*, 28, 40, 242.

22 Arendt, *Origins*, 33.

23 Arendt, *Origins*, xiv.

24 We shall address in a further chapter 'anti-Zionist' conceptions of the co-responsibility of Jews for antisemitism, which are wrongly associated with Arendt.

25 Arendt, *Jewish Writings*, 48.

26 Hannah Arendt, *Eichmann in Jerusalem: A Report on the Banality of Evil* (New York: Viking, 1965), 269.

27 Hannah Arendt, *Eichmann in Jerusalem*, 269.

28 Arendt, *Jewish Writings*, 9.

29 Hannah Arendt, *Rahel Varnhagen: The Life of a Jewess*, ed. Liliane Weissberg (Baltimore, MD; London: Johns Hopkins University Press 1997), 256.

30 Arendt, *Jewish Writings*, 53.

31 Arendt, *Jewish Writings*, 48.

32 Arendt, *Jewish Writings*, 51.

33 Arendt, *Jewish Writings*, 52.

34 Arendt, *Jewish Writings*, 42.

35 Arendt, *Origins*, 80.

36 Arendt, *Jewish Writings*, 284.

37 Arendt, *Jewish Writings*, 275.

38 For a survey of 'pariah types', explaining why Lazare was Arendt's ideal type, see Tuija Parvikko, The Responsibility of the Pariah: The Impact of Bernard Lazare on Arendt's Conception of Political Action and Judgement in Extreme Situations (Finland: SoPhi Academic Press, 2000).

39 Arendt, *Jewish Writings*, 276.

40 Arendt, *Jewish Writings*, 283.

41 Staudenmaier, 'Hannah Arendt's Analysis of Antisemitism'.

42 See, for example, Shulamit Volkov, *Germans, Jews, and Antisemites: Trials in Emancipation* (Cambridge: Cambridge University Press, 2006); Steven E. Aschheim, *Scholem, Arendt, Klemperer: Intimate Chronicles in Turbulent Times* (Bloomington: Indiana

University Press 2001); George Mosse, *German Jews Beyond Judaism* ((Bloomington: Indiana University Press; Cincinnati, Hebrew Union College Press, 1985). It should be noted that the total of conversions in Vienna between 1868 and 1903 was about 9000 Jews, less than 10% of the whole. Even this was proportionately higher than that for Berlin. See Jacques Le Rider, *Modernity and Crises of Identity: Culture and Society in Fin-de-Siècle Vienna*, trans. Rosemary Morris (New York: Continuum, 1993), 187–204.

43 According to Le Rider, the journalist and writer Karl Kraus attacked assimilationism from the other side: 'why attack the antisemites when it was Jewish and liberal corruption in finance and the press that was causing all the trouble?', *Modernity and Crises of Identity*, 252.

44 Arendt, 'What Remains?'

45 Arendt, *Jewish Writings*, 48.

46 Arendt, *Jewish Writings*, 75.

47 Arendt, *Jewish Writings*, 137.

48 Arendt, *Origins*, 272. On this striking convergence, see Eric Hobsbawm, *Nations and Nationalism since 1780*, second edition (Cambridge: Cambridge University Press, 1992).

49 Arendt *Origins*, 301–302. Arendt was preoccupied by the emergence of a stateless class of human beings, numbered in millions, expelled from their homes, turned into refugees, confronted by police blocking access into other countries, and their predicament ascribed to their own natural deficiencies. This transformation of the European landscape profoundly affected Jewish minorities, many of whom were driven westward as stateless refugees. Often this meant that Jews were persecuted by local nationalists before being hunted down by Nazis. It was, in part, because Arendt was exercised by the plight of Jews in Europe, that she supported attempts to build a Jewish democratic state in Palestine. On the role of nationalists in murdering Jews, see Snyder, *Black Earth* and Aristotle Kallis, *Genocide and Fascism: The Eliminationist Drive in Fascist Europe* (Abingdon: Ashgate, 2009).

50 Arendt, *Jewish Writings*, 336.

51 Arendt, *Jewish Writings*, 364–365.

52 Arendt, *Jewish Writings*, 364.

53 Arendt, *Jewish Writings*, 372.

54 Arendt, *Jewish Writings*, 427.

55 Arendt, *Jewish Writings*, 430.

56 Arendt, *Jewish Writings*, 428.

57 In recent discussions of Arendt's Jewish writings, some contemporary radical readers of her work misconstrue Arendt's critique of Zionism as a forerunner of the contemporary 'antizionism' of which they are advocates. In our judgment they underplay the significance of Arendt's critique of assimilationism and her support for the establishment of Israel. See, for example, Judith Butler, *Parting Ways; Jewishness and the Critique of Zionism* (New York: Columbia University Press, 2014); Jacqueline Rose, *The Question of Zion* (Princeton, NJ; Oxford: Princeton University Press 2005).

58 The category of 'crimes against humanity' was conceived in 1945 to enable prosecution of the kind of crimes Eichmann was accused of but was marginalised in practice

in the Nuremburg Trials. See Donald Bloxham, *Genocide on Trial: War Crimes Trials and the Formation of Holocaust History and Memory* (Oxford: Oxford University Press, 2001). The Genocide Convention of 1948 was formulated in part as a response to the Holocaust, but the history of genocidal antisemitism did not figure prominently in discussions of the Convention or in the final text. Arendt's determination to write about the Eichmann trial was triggered by the fact that the prosecution of a key architect and administrator of the 'final solution' directly raised the human meaning of genocidal antisemitism.

59 At one point Arendt wrote rather hyperbolically of David Ben-Gurion, Prime Minister of Israel, that he was trying to turn the prosecution into a 'show trial'. However, the term 'show trial' conjures up a different phenomenon – the charging of people with crimes they did not commit, and murdering them in order to terrorise others. Neither applies to the Eichmann trial. It also seems to be the case that she exaggerated the effect that Ben-Gurion had on the construction of the prosecution and on its reception in Israel. See Hanna Yablonka, *The State of Israel vs. Adolf Eichmann* (New York: Schocken Books, 2004).

60 Arendt emphasised that the category 'crimes against humanity' was not just a juridical name, but an accurate way of capturing the radical project of eradicating the idea of humanity. The relation of the concept to actuality is discussed in her correspondence with Jaspers around both the Nuremberg and Eichmann trials and in *Eichmann in Jerusalem*. See, for example, 268–269. See Robert Fine, 'Crimes Against Humanity: Hannah Arendt and the Nuremberg Debates', *European Journal of Social Theory*, 3 (3), 2000: 293–311.

61 Hannah Arendt, 'Organised Guilt and Universal Responsibility' in Hannah Arendt, *Essays in Understanding 1930–1954* (New York: Harcourt Brace, 1994), 131–132.

62 Arendt, *Eichmann in Jerusalem*, 273.

63 Arendt also raised the importance of introducing a third element into cosmopolitan ways of thinking: not only universalism and particularism but also uniqueness, singularity, a deeper sense of plurality than is possible through the idea of common humanity or that of particular identity.

64 For Hitler's representation of universalism as a 'Jewish idea' that had to be destroyed see Snyder, *Black Earth*, 5–6; and 'Hitler's World', *New York Review of Books*, 63 (14), 24 September to 7 October 2015: 6–10.

65 Gershom Scholem, 'Letter to Arendt 1963' in Hannah Arendt, *The Jew as Pariah*, ed. Ron Feldman (New York: Grove Press, 1978), 241.

66 Hannah Arendt 'Letter to Scholem 1963' in Arendt, *Jew as Pariah*, 247 and Arendt, *Jewish Writings*, 466–467.

67 Arendt, *Origins*, 73.

68 Arendt, *Origins*, 74.

69 Arendt, *Jewish Writings*, 467.

70 Malachi Haim Hacohen writes that the philosopher Karl Popper 'spoke little of the Jewish predicament' but 'rejected all nationalism, German and Jewish alike. The Open Society offered a radical cosmopolitan alternative to Central European nationalism'. He spoke of Jews as exemplary cosmopolitans as well as citizens in their respective countries. He deconstructed the nation state but 'never extended this mode

of questioning to the old Austro-Hungarian Empire ... The gap between cosmopolitan dream and ethnonational realities came back to haunt Popper with a vengeance'. Franz Kafka commented perceptively in this vein in a letter to Brod, 1921: 'Most [Jewish writers] who began writing in German wanted to distance themselves from Jewishness ... but their hind legs were still stuck to their father's Jewishness and their forelegs found no new ground'. See Malachi Haim Hacohen, 'Popper's Cosmopolitanism' in Steven Beller, *Rethinking Vienna 1900* (Oxford: Berghahn, 2001), 171–194. Arendt comments critically on Stephan Zweig's aloofness from his Jewishness and on his inability to reconcile himself to the fact that 'the famous Stephan Zweig had become the Jew Zweig'. See Hannah Arendt, *Reflections on Literature and Culture*, ed. Susannah Young-ah Gottlieb (Stanford: Stanford University Press, 2007), 59. Zweig was often asked to lend his voice to anti-Nazi and Jewish causes, but by his own admission he was anything but outspoken. Arendt argued that Zweig clung to the hope that, if he didn't draw attention to himself, his work could somehow continue unimpeded. Klaus Mann was no less disparaging of Zweig's decision to remain 'objective', 'understanding', and 'just' toward the deadly enemy.

71 Arendt, *Jewish Writings*, 282. Arendt lauded the Soviet Union as a country in which the rights of Jews were guaranteed by constitutional law and the penal code. She was wholly mistaken. Her central point, however, stands – that it is not a moral or political failure to struggle against antisemitism as one form of the universal struggle against oppression and exploitation.

72 Cited in Jacques Le Rider, 'The Assimilated Jews of Vienna' in Le Rider, *Modernity and Crises of Identity*, 200. Le Rider points out that the Jewish writer, Stefan Zweig, was misled by his own 'almost unreasoning cosmopolitanism'. After hailing Emile Verhaeren as a 'pan-European', he was 'shattered to discover in 1914 that his Belgian idol was an anti-German patriot, capable ... of violently antisemitic pronouncements' (200–201).

73 The erasure of any sign of Jews in favour of generic constructs like 'victims of Nazism' or 'anti-fascists' was common practice in official Communist memorials to the camps and has provided the template in which the mention of Jewish victims has been described as privileging the particularistic concerns of Jews. For a journalistic discussion see, for example, James Kirchick, 'The Holocaust without Jews', *Tablet*, 3 May 2016, www.tabletmag.com/jewish-news-and-politics/201420/the-holocaust-without-jews (accessed 3 June 2016).

74 Arendt, *Jewish Writings*, 466.

75 Hannah Arendt, *Lectures on Kant's Political Philosophy*, ed. Ronald Beiner (Chicago: University of Chicago Press, 1989), 75–76.

76 In *The Rebel* Albert Camus wrote in praise of rebellious moderation against absolutism: 'Moderation is not the opposite of rebellion. Rebellion in itself is moderation, and it demands, defends and recreates it throughout history ... Moderation, born of rebellion, can only live by rebellion'. See Albert Camus, *The Rebel* (Harmondsworth: Penguin, 2000), 301. We find something in Arendt's phenomenology of Jewish responsiveness to antisemitism that has close parallels with Camus' identity of rebellion and moderation.

5

The Jewish question after the Holocaust: Jürgen Habermas and the European left

I have, of course, long since abandoned my anti-Zionism, which was based on a confidence in the European labour movement, or, more broadly, in European society and civilisation, which that society and civilisation have not justified. If, instead of arguing against Zionism in the 1920s and 1930s I had urged European Jews to go to Palestine, I might have helped to save some of the lives that were later extinguished in Hitler's gas chambers. For the remnants of European Jewry – is it only for them? – the Jewish State has become an historic necessity. (Isaac Deutscher, *The Reporter* 1954)[1]

The Holocaust becomes a sort of university, an educational experience – a great learning experience, you might say – from which Jews were ethically obliged to have graduated with First Class Honours. But Israel, and those Jews who support Israel, are the overwhelming proof that they flunked their studies. ... Thus are Jews doubly damned: to the Holocaust itself and to the moral wasteland of having found no humanising redemption in its horrors. (Howard Jacobson, *When will Jews be Forgiven for the Holocaust?*)[2]

After the Holocaust, European antisemitism did not simply vanish like a puff of smoke. On her return to Germany in 1950 Hannah Arendt wrote of the resentment some 'ordinary Germans' felt for being blamed for Auschwitz. It was as if the real culprits were Jews who exploited the Holocaust for their own benefit, made money out of their suffering, denied the right of Germans to express their own suffering, and accused the Germans of being uniquely evil in their treatment of others.[3] In 1959 Theodor Adorno deployed the term 'secondary antisemitism' to conceptualise the opinion he found not uncommon within Germany that the Jewish people were culpable of exploiting German guilt over the Holocaust.[4] It was not only in Germany that Jewish survivors met with indifference and hostility. Some survivors spoke of the reluctance of their fellow human beings to hear the story of their experiences; some told of the hostility they faced when they tried to return to their old homes; some told of the official restrictions imposed on them by Western governments.[5] On the other side of the Iron Curtain, new regimes in Eastern Europe presented the nations they ruled as victims of National Socialism, not as perpetrators against Jews, and official antisemitic campaigns were planned and conducted in the Soviet Union and its satellite countries in the name of extirpating Zionism and cosmopolitanism.[6] The historian Tony Judt summarised the issue very well when he commented that 'what is truly awful about the destruction of the Jews is not that it mattered so much but that it mattered so little'.[7]

There were exceptions to this norm.[8] The enactment of 'crimes against humanity' and two further founding documents of the postwar epoch, the Genocide Convention and the Universal Declaration of Human Rights, passed in1948 within 24 hours of each other, were all informed by the common sense that human beings need protection from the violence of which the modern state has shown itself capable. These were very important innovations in International Criminal Law. They represented, as Karl Jaspers put it, the hint of a cosmopolitanism to come – 'a feeble, ambiguous harbinger of a world order the need of which mankind is beginning to feel'.[9] However, they were considerably marginalised with the onset of the Cold War. In 1960–1961 consciousness of the destruction of the Jews took an arguably more national form in the trial of Adolf Eichmann and then with the re-conceptualisation of the 'final solution to the Jewish question' (the Nazi formulation) as the 'Holocaust' (a Greek word for a burnt sacrificial offering) or 'Shoah' (a Hebrew word for destruction or catastrophe). In the 1980s, consciousness of the enormity of the event itself – and of German and European culpability – found public expression in narratives told in books, films and television series and in the spread of official apologies, commemoration sites, Holocaust museums and laws criminalising Holocaust denial.[10] The fall of the Berlin Wall in 1989 drew some former satellite countries of the Soviet bloc into the orbit of Holocaust commemoration. The Holocaust, Shoah, Auschwitz – these names became universal references for radical evil and the barbarism of our age.[11]

The difficulties of understanding the wilful destruction of a whole people, addressed by the old generation of critical theorists under the immediate shadow of the Holocaust, also shaped the political thought of critical theory's leading postwar representative, Jürgen Habermas. Habermas sought to face up to the legacy of genocidal antisemitism by addressing its connections with the rise of emphatically nationalistic forms of political community and by crafting a vision of postnational political community as the normative potential of our age. One of the markers of critical theory, as Habermas understood it, was to recognise that overcoming antisemitism lies at the centre of any worthwhile project of European reconstruction.[12]

Jürgen Habermas: antisemitism and the postnational project

Habermas conceived the postnational constellation as a multi-layered global order, consisting of a reformed basis of solidarity *within* the nation state, the development of new transnational forms of political community such as the European Union *beyond* the nation state, and the enhancement of international laws and institutions regulating relations between states and guaranteeing human rights at the *global* level. The idea of the postnational constellation entailed a differentiated and multi-layered architectonic of legal and political forms, as well as a complex re-invigoration of cosmo-political ways of thinking and acting in the world. Habermas presented the postnational constellation both as a desirable idea for the future and as a contested but tangible social reality in the present. We see it as a response both to the top-down forms of state socialism advanced within orthodox Marxism, and to the populist principle that all political life *must derive exclusively from below.*

The struggle to work through the experience of antisemitism was a vital element in this overall project. Habermas' guiding intuition was that antisemitism was the product of emphatically nationalist forms of political community and that postnationalism could introduce a new political order in which the conditions that once gave rise to antisemitism would no longer exist. He emphasised the modernity of antisemitism, rooting it in the perverted forms of nationalism the modern age is prone to generate.

The key issue, as Habermas saw it, is that the *Volksnation*, the nation of the people, was a modern democratic invention which crystallised into 'an efficient mechanism for repudiating everything regarded as foreign, for devaluing other nations, and for excluding national, ethnic, and religious minorities, especially the Jews. In Europe, nationalism became allied with antisemitism, with disastrous consequences'.[13] Habermas maintained that the historical strength of nationalism was due to its capacity to act as a binding power enabling individuals to coalesce around commonly shared symbols, and that the formation of the modern state was dependent on the development of a national consciousness to provide it with the cultural substrate for civil solidarity: 'only a national consciousness crystallised around the notion of a common ancestry, language and history, only the consciousness of belonging to "the same" people, makes subjects into citizens of a single political community – into members who can feel responsible for one another'.[14]

For Habermas, the nation state is a Janus-faced phenomenon characterised above all by normative ambiguity: it did become the bearer of a regressive credo that unreflectively celebrates the history, destiny, culture or blood of a nation, but it could also be the bearer of a progressive and inclusive form of political consciousness, which Habermas called 'constitutional patriotism' and understood as a consciousness capable of inspiring *rational* loyalty on the part of citizens.[15] Habermas maintained that some kind of national consciousness is needed to inculcate willingness on the part of citizens to do what is required of them for the common good, such as maintaining public services through taxation and accepting democratic decisions as legitimate, and that the virtue of constitutional patriotism is to perform these integrative functions in ways that do not exclude people deemed not worthy of belonging to the nation in question. Constitutional patriotism seemed to bridge the gap between shared attachment towards *universalistic* principles and the actualisation of these principles through *particular* national institutions. Habermas did not reject the national aspect but sought to render it benign through the harmonisation of the universal and the particular.

Habermas' concession to nationalism suggested by his conceptual approach to constitutional patriotism became more pronounced when the concept was applied in practice to Germany. He adopted constitutional patriotism as an antidote to German ethnic nationalism and as a device to re-integrate the Federal Republic of Germany and later a united Germany as a pluralistic, multicultural political community. He deployed the idea very effectively as a critical resource against the resurgence of ethnic nationalism he saw in the 'Historians Debate' of the 1980s. He criticised one historian (Michael Stürmer) for celebrating the 'higher source of meaning' that only nationalism could provide; another (Andreas Hillgruber) for identifying with 'the desperate and costly struggle of the German army in the East [...] who were trying to save the population of the German East from the Red Army's orgies of revenge', a third (Ernst Nolte) for normalising Auschwitz as a response to a 'more original Asiatic deed', that of the Gulag.[16] Habermas maintained, by contrast, that German national identity could only be rebuilt on the basis of a joint responsibility for the past, carried over into next generations, so that the dead would not be cheated out of the 'memory of the sufferings of those who were murdered by German hands'. It was not resurgent nationalism but the liberating power of 'reflective remembrance' that could rebuild German identity.[17]

Habermas was not prepared to dissolve the murder of *Jews* into some universal reference to the victims of Nazism, as Soviet Marxism insisted. In a discussion of the Berlin Holocaust memorial in *Die Zeit* in 1999, he criticised the argument that 'exclusive reference to the murdered Jews now reflects a particularism that ignores the victims of other groups' or that it represents 'an injustice to the Sinti and Roma, the political prisoners, the mentally handicapped, the homosexuals, the Jehovah's Witnesses and the deserters which demands some redress'. He acknowledged that the moral intuition to which this universalism appealed was powerful and that the special 'significance of the Jews for us Germans must not neutralise the unconditional obligation to show equal respect in commemorating all victims', but he could not accept a line of argument that seemed to him universalistic only in the abstract. He wrote: 'Were we to ignore the special relevance of the Jews for the social and cultural life of Germany, the historically fraught, quite specific proximity and distances of both these unequal poles, wouldn't we once again be guilty of a false abstraction?'[18] Habermas understood that there is no contradiction between attending to the genocide of Jews and drawing universalistic ethical conclusions. To focus on the genocide of one particular people is not to sign up to particularism.[19] Quite the reverse: we learn to generalise from particular cases and, if required, to allow new cases to modify our generalisations.[20]

A more problematic aspect of Habermas' argument was the role played by 'the German question' in his approach. Habermas presented Germany as a model for Europe as a whole on the grounds that the trend toward postnational self-understanding was more pronounced there than in any other European state. Germany appeared as the nation that, by virtue of learning from its past excesses, now most fully acknowledged ethnic nationalism as a horrific regression.[21] It was as if Germany, above all European nations, had the reflective resources required for a genuinely 'critical appropriation of ambiguous traditions'. Habermas treated Germany as a normative model for postnational political community on the grounds that in Germany nationalism was no longer normatively defensible.[22] He articulated very well the normative content of the postnational ideal – rejection of nationalism; loyalty to constitutional principles; cultivation of a reflective consciousness; ability to relativise one's own way of life; granting strangers the same rights as ourselves; recognising the heterogeneity of populations, including all citizens regardless of origin, colour, creed, or language, etc. – but he was tempted to represent Germany as the privileged site of this ideal.[23] Habermas traded on an ambiguity between two distinct propositions – that constitutional patriotism was a desirable goal for German reconstruction, and that Germany was already an exemplary case of constitutional patriotism. His own resolution was to say that constitutional patriotism operates in a space 'between facts and norms', that it walks a tightrope between what is and what it might be, but this formulation still enables reversion from his original commitment to work through the catastrophe to the fixed idea that Germany has in fact learnt the lessons of the catastrophe it caused.[24] The postnational approach Habermas put forward opened a space for those who wish to situate the problem of German antisemitism emphatically in the past.

If the German rendition of constitutional patriotism left it uncomfortably close to a new kind of nationalism, this was one reason why Habermas turned to a wider European stage. He was well aware that while there was a specific German responsibility, genocidal antisemitism was a phenomenon that found support in nearly all European countries, not only in Germany. Habermas emphasised the responsibility of all Europeans to commemorate the victims – primarily for the sake of the victims themselves but additionally as a means of 'reassuring ourselves [i.e. all Europeans] of our own political identity'. He endeavoured to keep in mind 'the gruesome features of a century that "invented" the gas chambers, total war, state-sponsored genocide, and extermination camps', but at the same time not to become 'transfixed by the gruesomeness of the century', not to evade 'conscious assessment of the horror that finally culminated in [...] the annihilation of the Jews of Europe'.[25] This active stance toward the whole of Europe learning from the past has profoundly shaped Habermas' work.

The turn to Europe, however, also conjured up the spectre of a new national-ism writ large. The nationalistic temptation was the idea of Europe as a civilisa-tion whose normative values, civic traditions and forms of life made it peculiarly 'capable of learning' and 'consciously shaping itself through its political will'.[26] Habermas' anti-*gemeinschaftlich* image of Europe avoided construing European identity along essentialist lines, but there rested a tendency not only to advance a postnational project for Europe but also to represent Europe as the privileged site of postnationalism. The equivocations of postnationalism between a critical and positivist approach encouraged the belief that Europe has learnt its lessons and thus made it possible after all to 'historicise' antisemitism as a phenomenon of the past. One of the most paradoxical conclusions others have drawn from this idealised view of postnational Europe is that the only people deemed not to have learnt these lessons were the victims themselves!

This is not the road, however, that Habermas took. His postnational journey took a further step toward the reconstruction of world society and its global institutions, its international laws and its human rights. Habermas maintained that the normative effect of the 'monstrous mass crimes of the twentieth century' has been to acknowledge that 'states as the subjects of international law forfeited the presumption of innocence that underlies the prohibition on intervention and immunity against criminal prosecution under international law'.[27] He did not reject the principles of classical international law – self-determination of peoples, respect for treaties, non-intervention in the internal affairs of other peoples, agreed norms regulating the conduct of war – but emphasised the need to elabo-rate international law in accordance with more cosmopolitan principles: states are bound to honour human rights; the principle of non-intervention may be suspended in the case of serious atrocities; and the authority of international organisations such as the United Nations must be upheld. Habermas defended the *principle* that the international community has a legal as well as moral duty to intervene where and when states commit heinous crimes against the people and that atrocity-committing states should not be allowed to hide behind the fig leaf of national self-determination and non-interference. He laid the ground for a constitutionalised global order to come, incompatible with the order that once made the 'final solution' possible.

Habermas had the vision of constructing a fully-fledged legal framework to protect people from the violence of states. He hoped to realise this vision by extending the reach of global remedies, granting the International Court of Justice compulsory jurisdiction, sharpening the definition of humanitarian crimes, reforming the Security Council, constructing a UN army, and so forth. He acknowledged that this cosmopolitan vision was far from an accomplished fact: human rights interventions were fraught with difficulties, particular interests were dressed up in the universalistic rhetoric of international law, and indeed a culture of human rights had yet to be developed if social actors were to judge and act on political matters from the perspective of 'citizens of the world'.[28] His approach, however tended to concieve of change in ideal terms as a transition from a world in which law was in the service of power to a world in which power will be in the service of law, a formulation that did not address his own understanding of law as a form of power – witness the struggles for power waged for control of the institutional bodies through which human rights are enacted on the world stage. He defended the legitimacy of human rights bodies in terms of supplementing the functional capacities of nation states and tempering the temptation of powerful states to imagine themselves as all-powerful, but this defence did not address the legitimacy problems human rights themselves encounter in addressing social inequalities, regulating the aggression of state powers, matching the democratic validity possible at the national level, or resisting expropriation by corporate capital and state power. He argued that the limited democratic legitimacy of international institutions was justified by the limited functions they perform, rested on legal principles tried and tested within democratic constitutions, and received supplementary legitimacy through the activism of global civil society,[29] but this vindication of cosmopolitan law could not obscure the existence of a chasm between the abstract idea of universal human rights and concrete norms of social and political inequality.[30]

These problems were unresolved but the more troubling aspect of this stage of the postnational journey was that the idealisation of human rights made it possible to suspend the formal principle of equality between states and reconfigure a hierarchy of states based this time on human rights criteria. One such strategy was employed by the philosopher, John Rawls, when in the *Law of Peoples* he elevated to the top of this hierarchy of states those labelled 'liberal' that uphold *all* human rights, placed below them states labelled 'decent' that only respect *some* human rights, and placed at the bottom of the hierarchy states labelled 'outlaw' that respect *no* human rights at all.[31] While the classification of states according to human rights criteria was not part of Habermas' own project, the equivocations of postnationalism – caught between norms and facts, critical engagement and uncritical rationalisation – introduced an inegalitarian mindset into the very concept of international law. In the work of Rawls, this mindset became all the more pronounced when he substituted the category of 'peoples' for that of 'states'. His intention was that of emphasising equality under international law rather than absolute sovereignty, but it obscured the distinction between state and civil society and invited slippage from condemning a *state* for its human rights abuses to condemning a *people* on account of the human rights abuses committed by the state to which they belong. The erasure of this distinction between state and civil society opened a door to the admission of a stigmatising way of thinking in international law. The condemnation of a 'people' as a 'pariah nation' was not inherent in the postnational project but it did become a potentiality within it. One of the key relevancies of this turn was to offer a philosophical aperture through which it became possible to reinstate the Jewish question under a postnational or cosmopolitan banner.

The new radicalism and the deformations of critical theory

Habermas' postnational project was part of a magnificent intellectual and political movement, whose aim was to reconstruct the Enlightenment project for modern times and to develop the categories of understanding and standards of judgment needed to confront the barbarism of the modern age. Its main offering has been the development of a genuinely universalistic critique of European antisemitism as an integral part of its critical and emancipatory programme. It aimed to translate the slogans 'never again' and 'universal responsibility' into tangible, practical and enduring measures. Our contention, however, is that the successive idealisations we have sought to identify – nationalism writ benign in Germany, nationalism writ large in Europe, the absolutism of human rights as standard of judgment in world society, faith in the social learning Europe achieved through the Holocaust – all left cracks in the postnational edifice that allowed less critical forces to enter. Habermas himself cited Thomas Mann's aphorism in *Germany and the Germans* (1945) that there were 'not two Germanys, an evil and a good, but only one that through devil's cunning transformed its best into evil'.[32] If the devil's cunning can turn the best of modern civilisation into the worst, we should acknowledge the possibility that this can also be the fate of postnationalism itself. Like other forms of universalism, postnationalism can be abused to label others 'nationalist' or stigmatise others as its enemies. While postnationalism, as Habermas conceived it, had as its aim the supersession of the Jewish question and its replacement by a vista of Jewish emancipation appropriate to its time, the cracks in the postnational edifice allowed a different agenda to enter. It was to turn the Jewish nation into the 'other' of the postnational. The Jewish nation becomes in this version of the postnational project the personification of radical alterity.[33]

A distorted universalism of this type has become increasingly evident within the mainstreams of the contemporary political left, who are wholly opposed to antisemitism but who base their opposition on reconfiguring the very Jewish question that lay behind antisemitism in the first place. We can illustrate the kind of radicalism we have in mind with a few brief examples drawn from leading left intellectuals of the recent period. The historian Tony Judt wrote in the *New York Review of Books* that Holocaust memory crowded out all other injustices by treating the Holocaust not as one evil among many but as 'radical evil'. He maintained that the charge of antisemitism was being politically instrumentalised:

> Today, when Israel is exposed to international criticism for its mistreatment of Palestinians and its occupation of territory conquered in 1967, its defenders prefer to emphasise the memory of the Holocaust. If you criticise Israel too forcefully, they warn, you will awaken the demons of antisemitism. Indeed, they suggest, robust criticism of Israel doesn't just arouse antisemitism. It is antisemitism.[34]

The philosopher Judith Butler pursued the same line of argument when she expressed the view that 'the charge of anti-Semitism' was exercising a 'chilling effect on political discourse' and maintained that 'certain actions of the Israeli state – acts of violence and murder against children and civilians – must not be objected to … for fear that any protest against them would be tantamount to anti-Semitism'. She held that the 'charge of antisemitism' was being used to 'translate what one is actually hearing, a protest against the killing of children and civilians by the Israeli army, into nothing more than a cloak for hatred of Jews'.[35] The cultural historian Matti Bunzl contended that the focus on antisemitism deflects attention from the 'real racisms' coursing through postnational Europe, especially the Islamophobia fuelled by social forces that brought millions of Muslims to Europe and based on 'the notion that Islam engenders a world view that is fundamentally incompatible with and inferior to Western culture'.[36] The sociologist Goran Therborn wrote of the 'complete delegitimation of anti-Semitism in mainstream discourse after the discovery of the horrors of Auschwitz and the complete defeat of Nazi Germany' and maintained that the charge 'anti-Semite' has become a '*Totschlagwort*, a killing word … a lethal weapon in public polemics'. Maintaining that the word 'antisemitism' functions to dismiss 'fundamental critical questions about the state of Israel', he contrasted the old 'European time' in which he claims Israel still exists – time rooted in 'ethnic nationalism', 'divine right of Jews' and 'European atonement for the Holocaust' – with modern 'world time' that is supposedly rooted in 'de-colonization, universal rights, and the assertion and recognition of indigenous peoples and of non-European religions and cultures'.[37]

The Marxist philosopher Alain Badiou, who for many years continued to profess loyalty to Maoism and Pol Pot, has the virtue of articulating what is muted in others.[38] He condemns what he describes as a powerful and reactionary current in contemporary political life that speaks in the name of 'the Jews' and claims to see 'antisemitism everywhere' (*L'antisémitisme Partout* is the French title of a book he co-authored with Eric Hazan).[39] He maintains that this powerful and reactionary current has constructed a 'victim ideology' around the sign of 'the Jew', which renders other forms of victimisation invisible, demands that Israel's crimes be tolerated and accuses those who do not tolerate them (like Badiou himself) of antisemitism. He opines that 'purveyors of antisemitism' are not only on the side of Israel against Palestinians but on that of *all* repressive power against popular resistance. Badiou aligns himself to the tradition of universalism he traces back to St Paul's disconnection of Christianity from established Judaism, and from this 'universalistic' vantage point denounces 'Israel' as the placeholder for all that is hostile to the modern cosmopolitan and non-identitarian state.[40] He draws a parallel between the fact that 'Hitler once took power in the name of a politics whose categories included the term "Jew"' and the fact that Israel has taken power in the name of a politics whose categories also include the term 'Jew'.[41] He objects to the characterisation of the Nazi extermination of Jews as 'radical evil', on the grounds that it is thereby declared 'unthinkable, unsayable, without conceivable precedent or posterity', only to accuse Zionists of doing to Palestinians what the Nazis did to the Jews.[42]

The distorted form of universalism presents itself as a continuance of critical theory, but advances quite different propositions. First, it relegates antisemitism to the past. Its narrative is that the genocidal antisemitism that once stalked Europe has been discredited and marginalised by the horror it generated and that no new forms of antisemitism have emerged. Hostility to what is called 'new antisemitism theory' is its informing passion. Second, it claims a radical dissociation of antisemitism from other forms of racism. Its narrative here is that in the past people of colour and people of Jewish background may have been 'brothers in misery' and that antisemitism and racism may have represented the 'same bankruptcy of man',[43] but that today Muslims have become the 'new Jews' and Islamophobia has become the 'new antisemitism'.[44] Third, it maintains that the universal significance of the Holocaust has been sacrificed to a particularism, which treats it only as an event in *Jewish* history and stigmatises other groups of people – be they Muslims, Arabs, Europeans or the left – as wholly antisemitic.[45] Finally, it disparages the motives of those who raise concerns about antisemitism, on the grounds that 'they' abuse collective memory and the charge of antisemitism for clandestine ends – for instance, to discredit critics of Israel or pathologise victims of Israeli power. The mark of this distorted form of universalism is to treat the problem of antisemitism as unserious compared with that of raising antisemitism as a problem.

The elements of this new 'critical theory' – emphatic historicisation of antisemitism, dissociation of racism and antisemitism, particularisation of Holocaust commemovation, a cynical reading of resistance to antisemitism – demonstrate that while it claims to oppose antisemitism in the name of a universalistic ethos, its conviction is that antisemitism is a problem of the past, that to focus on it in the present is an anachronism, that the priority of contemporary antiracism should lie with other racisms, that opposition to antisemitism has been consumed by a damaging particularism, and that a conspiratorial agenda lies behind the charge of antisemitism. We are confronted here by a discourse that subverts the universalism it espouses by turning the signifier 'Jew' into its other. In place of the deep and careful reflections we find in critical theory on what overcoming antisemitism requires, we find ourselves once again in the grip of the Jewish question. All formulations of the Jewish question come back to the harm 'the Jews' allegedly inflict on humanity at large and what is to be done about this harm. Its contemporary reconfiguration gives it a more symbolic edge. The question is no longer posed about 'the Jews' as a race apart but rather about those who invoke the sign of 'the Jews' in order to *imagine* themselves as a race apart. Its concern is over the harm caused to humanity by those who invoke the word 'Jew' in the lexicon of self-identity – be it the Jewish state, the Jewish nation, Jewish collective memory, or even Jewish opposition to antisemitism – and the need to find solutions to the harm they cause. The Enlightenment credo that 'we must refuse everything to the Jews as a nation and accord everything to Jews as individuals', re-emerges as a discourse valuing Jews as individuals but correspondingly open to the devaluation of Jews as a nation.

The key defect of this discourse does not lie in its theoretical claim to universalism but in the ways it belies these claims in practice. There are doubtless *some* individuals and groups who combat antisemitism from a more or less particularistic point of view but there are so many others who – in the tradition of Marx, Horkheimer, Adorno and Arendt – see antisemitism as an occasion to raise universal issues concerning what it is to be human in the modern age and who seek answers to how humanity in its diversity can be protected. A cursory review of the Holocaust Memorial Day Trust website reveals the many connections it has drawn between the Holocaust and other genocides.[46] While Holocaust commemoration addresses the murder and suffering of Jews or of those defined as Jews, its focus on the particulars of Jewish suffering emphatically does not entail a *particularism* unconcerned with the sufferings of others. The apparently universalistic demand advanced by some critics of Holocaust Memorial Day, that it be replaced by a Genocide Memorial Day, demonstrates its own resentment of any focus on *Jewish* suffering in the claim that 'the Jews' overstate what was done to *them*.[47] It is resonant of how the annihilation of Jews was subsumed in the Soviet Union to generic formulations concerning 'victims of Nazism' and with the collapse of Communism in East Europe to generic formulations like 'victims of Stalinism'.[48] Concern over particulars is not to be confused with particularism or, to put the matter another way, it is a bogus universalism that represses the particular.

It is a common characteristic of groups subjected to racism to resist racism from a nationalist point of view. Nothing may appear more natural, as Arendt once remarked, than that if you are attacked as a Jew, you may well fight back as a Jew. The same may be said for any other category: if you are attacked as a Black or a Muslim, you may well fight back as a Black or a Muslim. While Arendt saw the national character of resistance to racism and antisemitism as a limitation, within some sections of the Marxist tradition the 'nationalism of the oppressed' has long been advanced as the *ideal* form of struggle against the racism of oppressors. Cosmopolitan thinking addresses the determinate character of nationalism as a form of resistance to racism but it is the echo of an old prejudice to heap upon *Jewish* nationalism the defects of nationalism in general. Similarly, we may acknowledge that the 'charge of antisemitism' can be instrumentalised on behalf of particular interests, but so too can any charge of racism. The scent of old prejudice is present if instrumentalism, self-interest and deceit are turned into the kernel of the 'charge of antisemitism'. Of course it is undesirable to resist antisemitic abstractions of 'the Jews' by means of equally homogenising typifica-tions of 'the Muslims' or 'the French' or 'the left' as antisemitic. The sociologist Raymond Aron sought to capture the nature of this reversal in a discussion of Jean Paul Sartre's *Antisemite and Jew*:

> Anti-antisemites tend to present all the colonisers, all the antisemites, all the whites as essentially defined by their contempt for natives, hatred of Jews, desire for segregation. They paint a portrait of the coloniser, the antisemite or the whites that is as totalising as their stereotypes of the Jew, the native or the Blacks. The antisemite must be *wholly* antisemitic.[49]

The cycle of inversion is merely repeated, however, if those who express concern about the rise of a new antisemitism are themselves treated as a homogeneous category defined by their collective stigmatisation of others.

The spirit of critical theory

We have argued that the array of concepts Habermas put forward for the recon-struction of political community, both in Europe and worldwide – constitutional patriotism, postnationalism, civic ethos, human rights, cosmopolitanism, etc. – provides us with universalistic means of combating antisemitism, but that they have been re-deployed in ways that corrode their critical content from within. The process of learning from catastrophe Habermas looked to has been converted into the fixed idea that antisemitism belongs only to the past. The valid distinction between nationalism and postnationalism has been turned into a categorical opposition that stigmatises Jewish expressions of national-ism and represents Holocaust memory as culpably nationalistic. In place of a critical theory in which the legacy of European antisemitism is centre stage, we encounter resistance to the notion that antisemitism is any longer a problem for Europe or that a new antisemitism can possibly arise. In place of combating antisemitism, we find suspicion of the motives of those who believe that it has arisen anew and ought to be combatted.

Stripping postnationalism of its critical content has not been the work of Habermas himself. If the project is to be blamed, it is only for the cracks in the postnational architectonic that have enabled others to reconfigure the Jewish question under a progressive, universalistic mantel. What we can say is that the reconfiguration of the Jewish question raises issues that Habermas has understandably not kept his eye on. Perhaps this explains his 'fright' when he was personally confronted with concerns about a new antisemitism coming not from the right but from the left. He recommended for publication a book by a Marxist philosopher who drew certain conclusions about the conflict in Israel-Palestine that Habermas did not share: notably in his failure to 'distinguish political evaluation of Palestinian terrorism from the moral justification of it'.[50] Habermas wrote that the author had made generalising statements that made him 'groan slightly', statements like the following: 'Having been the principal victims of racism in history, Jews now seem to have learned from their abusers'.[51] In response to a letter charging the book with antisemitism Habermas wrote that he did not agree: 'Sentences like this can always be used for antisemitic purposes, even against the author's intention, if they are taken out of context'. At the same time he qualified his own disagreement thus: 'I can well understand the reasons and fears of an apparently large section of our Jewish population. [...] If I have offended these feelings by my recommendation of this book, I am sorry'.[52] Whether or not we agree with Habermas' judgment in this case, the spirit of his engagement with the legacy of European antisemitism contrasts markedly with the purported radicalism of those who also claim to oppose antisemitism but whose universalism is actually deployed to bring the Jewish question back in.

Notes

1 Isaac Deutcher, *The Reporter* 1954, scanned and prepared for the Marxist Internet Archive by Paul Flewers, www.marxists.org/archive/deutscher/1954/israel.htm (accessed 7 October 2015). See also Martyn Hudson, 'Revisiting Isaac Deutscher', *Fathom*, Winter 2014, http://fathomjournal.org/revisiting-isaac-deutscher (accessed 14 November 215). For a different view, Samuel Farber, 'Isaac Deutscher and the Jews: An Analysis and Personal Reflection', *New Politics*, 14 (4), Winter 2014, http://newpol.org/content/deutscher-and-jews (accessed 15 December 2015).

2 Howard Jacobson, *When will Jews be Forgiven for the Holocaust?* (Kindle Single, 2014).

3 Hannah Arendt, 'The Aftermath of Nazi Rule: Report from Germany' in Arendt, *Essays in Understanding 1930–1954*, 248–269.

4 See Clemens Heni 'Secondary Antisemitism: From Hard-Core to Soft-Core Denial of the Shoah', *Jewish Political Studies Review*, 20, Fall 2008: 3–4.

5 Primo Levi recounted this nightmare in his Auschwitz memoir, *If This is a Man*, and then encountered something like it when he took the manuscript of *Se questo è un uomo* to the Italian publisher Einaudi in 1946 and it was rejected. For a wide-ranging study of the sustained hostility Jews faced, see David Bankier (ed.), *The Jews Are Coming Back: The Return of Jews to their Countries of Origin after WW2* (Oxford: Berghahn, 2005).

6 Stalin's ideologues were perhaps the first to suggest a correspondence between what the Nazis did to Jews and what Zionists did to Palestinians. See Zvi Gitelman 'The Soviet Union' in David S. Wyman and Charles H. Rosenzveig (eds.), *The World Reacts to the Holocaust* (Baltimore, Maryland: Johns Hopkins University Press, 1996), 295–324.

7 Tony Judt writes: 'The returning remnant was not much welcomed. After years of antisemitic propaganda, local populations everywhere were not only disposed to blame "Jews" in the abstract for their suffering, but were distinctly sorry to see the return of men and women whose jobs, possessions and apartments they had purloined … The choice for most of Europe's Jews seemed stark: depart … or else be silent and so far as possible invisible'. *Postwar: A History of Europe since 1945* (London: Pimlico, 2007), 804–807.

8 As we have seen, the architects of the Nuremberg trials conceived the category 'crimes against humanity' as an original attempt to deal legally with the destruction of European Jewry. While this charge was included in some of the indictments, the focus of the trials was on crimes against peace, and war crimes not directly connected with the Holocaust. In some cases Jewish witnesses were excluded from the proceedings. See Bloxham, *Genocide on Trial*. The charge of crimes against humanity had been used in a case made against the Ottoman regime by the Allies in 1915, but it did not form part of the feeble attempt to prosecute the perpetrators of the genocide of the Armenians after the First World War. See Fine, 'Crimes against Humanity', 293–311.

9 Karl Jaspers, *The Question of German Guilt* (New York: Capricorn, 1961), 60.

10 Holocaust denial evolved together with Holocaust commemoration. See Deborah Lipstadt, *Denying the Holocaust: The Growing Assault on Truth and Memory* (New York: Plume, 1994). On memorialisation, see James E. Young, *The Texture of Memory: Memorials and Meaning in Europe, Israel, and America* (New Haven: Yale University Press 1993). Concerning efforts to outlaw Holocaust denial and how they then generated further efforts to ban denial of other genocides, see Ludovic Hennebel and Thomas Hochmann (eds.), *Genocide Denials and the Law* (New York: Oxford University Press, 2011).

11 A discussion of the ways in which the Holocaust became a 'moral universal' is to be found in Jeffrey Alexander, *Remembering the Holocaust: A Debate* (Oxford; New York: Oxford University Press, 2009).

12 Our argument about Habermas' engagement with antisemitism draws in part from Robert Fine, 'Nationalism, Postnationalism, Antisemitism: Thoughts on the Politics of Jürgen Habermas', *Österreichische Zeitschrift Für Politikwissenschaft*, Special issue on 'Antisemitismus und die Transformation des Nationalen', ed. Karin Stoegner 2010, 4: 409–420.

13 Jürgen Habermas, *The Inclusion of the Other* (Cambridge, MA: MIT Press, 1998), 111.

14 Habermas, *The Inclusion of the Other*, 113.

15 Jürgen Habermas, *The Postnational Constellation: Political Essays*, ed. Max Pensky (Cambridge: Polity, 2001), 64. For further discussion of the normative ambiguity of the nation state, see Daniel Chernilo, *A Social Theory of the Nation State: The Political Forms of Modernity Beyond Methodological Nationalism* (London: Routledge, 2007), esp. 156.

16 Jürgen Habermas, *The New Conservatism: Cultural Criticism and the Historians Debate*, ed. Shierry Weber Nicholsen (Cambridge: Polity, 1991), 215–224.

17 Jürgen Habermas, *Autonomy and Solidarity: Interviews with Jürgen Habermas*, ed. Peter Dews (London: Verso, 1992), 240.

18 Jürgen Habermas, *Time of Transitions* (Cambridge: Polity, 2006), 48–49.

19 See Michael Rothberg, *Multidirectional Memory: Remembering the Holocaust in the Age of Decolonization* (Stanford, CA: Stanford University Press, 2009).

20 Robert Stake, *The Art of Case Study Research* (London: Sage, 1995), 85.

21 There is some force to this argument if we consider Angela Merkel's relatively open and hospitable reception of refugees in Germany recently, when compared to the resistance of other European states.

22 Habermas, *Time of Transition*, 47. Charles Turner shrewdly observes that Habermas' approach to nationalism appeared less persuasive to those nations whose recent history was one of national suppression, especially Eastern European nations seeking freedom from Russian rule. In Central and Eastern Europe 'the source of pain was not "nationalist excess" alone but rather six years of Nazi occupation followed by forty years of Soviet domination'. See Charles Turner, 'Jürgen Habermas: European or German?' *European Journal of Political Theory*, 3 (3), 2004: 293–314, at 303. Perhaps for Habermas the difference in experience between East and West is one reason why a united Germany is special.

23 See for example Robert Fine, 'The New Nationalism and Democracy: A Critique of *Pro Patria*', *Democratization*, 1 (3), 1994: 423–443. Habermas' distinction between constitutional patriotism and nationalism is not a million miles from the distinction between civic and ethnic nationalism. These distinctions are indeed significant but should not be allowed to obscure what is shared between them and how one can slide into the other. See Philip Spencer and Howard Wollman, *Nationalism: A Critical Introduction*, ch. 4 'Good and Bad Nationalisms' (London: Sage, 2002).

24 Jürgen Habermas, *Between Facts and Norms* (Cambridge: Polity 1997).

25 Jürgen Habermas, 'Learning from Catastrophe' in Habermas, *The Postnational Constellation*, 45.

26 Jürgen Habermas, *The Inclusion of the Other: Studies in Political Theory*, eds. Ciaran Cronin and Pablo de Greif (Cambridge, MA: MIT Press, 1998), 124.

27 Jürgen Habermas, 'The Constitutionalisation of International Law and the Legitimation Problems of a Constitution for World Society', *Constellations*, 15, 2008: 444–455, at 444.

28 For elaboration of the dangers of dressing up hegemonic power in the cloth of international law, see Jean Cohen, 'Whose Sovereignty? Empire Versus International Law', *Ethics and International Affairs*, 18 (3), 2004: 1–24, at 10.

29 Jürgen Habermas, *The Divided West* (Cambridge: Polity, 2006).

30 The outstanding analysis of the normative underpinnings of international law and of the legitimacy crisis into which it has entered is to be found in Hauke Brunkhorst, *Critical Theory of Legal Revolutions: Evolutionary Perspectives* (London: Bloomsbury, 2014).

31 John Rawls, *Law of Peoples* (London: Harvard University Press, 2001).

32 'Germany and the Germans' in *Thomas Mann's Addresses Delivered at the Library of Congress, 1942–1949* (Rockville, Maryland: Wildside Press, 2008), 45–66.

33 In our view, though this would take us far from our immediate topic, Islamophobia is not the 'new antisemitism' but is a phenomenon concurrent with the actual new antisemitism. The theorists and practitioners of Islamophobia and antisemitism are occasionally the same people, though far more often they are not, but both may be seen as unwanted offspring of the new universalism.

34 Tony Judt, 'The Problem of Evil in Postwar Europe', *New York Review of Books*, 552 (2), 14 February, 2008, www.nybooks.com/articles/2008/02/14/the-problem-of-evil-in-postwar-europe/ (accessed 24 July 2016).

35 Judith Butler, 'The Charge of Anti-Semitism: Jews, Israel and the Risks of Public Critique' in Judith Butler, *Precarious Life: The Powers of Mourning and Violence* (London: Verso 2004), 101. For Butler's 'Jewish' critique of Zionism see Seyla Benhabib, 'Ethics without Normativity and Politics without Historicity: On Judith Butler's Parting Ways – Jewishness and the Critique of Zionism', *Constellations*, 20 (1), March 2013: 150–163.

36 Matti Bunzl, *Antisemitism and Islamophobia: Hatreds Old and New in Europe* (Chicago: Prickly Paradigm Press, 2007), 13.

37 Göran Therborn 'Editorial: Three Epochs of European Anti-Semitism', *European Societies*, 14 (2), 161–165.

38 It is not easy to see why Badiou should be thought of as an authority on the question of state oppression. In 1968, at a time when the new and revolutionary left was as anti-Stalinist as it was anti-capitalist, Badiou was an enthusiastic supporter of the Cultural Revolution, then at its bloodiest. Ten years later, he wrote to *Le Monde* vigorously opposing the Vietnamese intervention in Cambodia, in spite of the fact that it put an end to one of the most catastrophic genocides in modern times when one third of the population was slaughtered. See Peter Hallward, *Badiou: A Subject to Truth* (Minneapolis, MN: University of Minnesota Press 2003). Hallward is one of the few writers on Badiou to acknowledge this record, conceding that 'this makes for painful retrospective reading' (*Badiou*, 413).

39 Alain Badiou, Eric Hazan and Ivan Segré, *Reflections on Antisemitism*, trans. David Fernbach (London: Verso, 2013). Originally in French, Alain Badiou and Eric Hazan, *L'Antisémitisme Partout: Aujourd'hui en France* (Paris: La Fabrique, 2011).

40 Alain Badiou 'The Uses of the Word "Jew"', trans. Steve Corcoran, www.lacan.com/badword.htm (accessed 30 November 2015). Badiou disregards the role of Pauline universalism in inaugurating the long history of anti-Judaism. For a scholarly account

of the anti-Judaic aspects of Pauline universalism and the toxic tradition it inaugurated, see Nirenberg, *Anti-Judaism* 48–87.

41 Badiou does not, as far as we know, address the contradiction between his *Ethics* in which he maintains that 'the real question' is not that of the 'right to difference' but rather that of 'recognizing the Same', and his politics in which he reconstructs an absolute division of the world between 'us' and 'them' in which there is no recognition of 'the Same'. Alain Badiou, *Ethics: An Essay on the Understanding of Evil*, trans. Peter Hallwood (London: Verso, 2002), 25.

42 While Badiou creates an association of ideas between Nazism and Zionism, he objects to the depiction by Western leaders of those 'against whom they act' (like Saddam Hussein or Slobodan Milosevic) as 'like Hitler' and points to the contradiction involved in saying that 'this crime is inimitable but every crime is an imitation of it'. See *Ethics*, 63.

43 Frantz Fanon, *The Wretched of the Earth*, trans. Constance Farrington (Harmondsworth: Penguin, 1967), 86.

44 Antisemitism is different in important respects from other forms of racism and Islamophobia, not least in its emphasis on Jews having secret and overwhelming control of the world, but competition of victimhood spawns unjustifiably different treatment of anti-antisemitism from other forms of antiracism. For example, the antiracist supposition that the voices of victims of racism should be carefully and empathetically heard is suspended in a politics of suspicion regarding voices of victims of antisemitism. See Cousin and Fine, 'Brothers in Misery, 308–324.

45 There are some who normalise the Holocaust by insisting it was of no greater significance than what was done by European colonialists and slave masters to generations of subjected peoples, except that the crime was mainly committed in Europe. It is said that 'preoccupation' with the Holocaust betrays a Eurocentrism that obscures the long history of racism and genocide on the part of Western imperialist states and that 'excessive' reference to the Holocaust obscures its relation to other genocides. See Vincent Pecora, 'Habermas, Enlightenment, and Antisemitism' in Saul Friedlander (ed.), *Probing the Limits of Representation: Nazism and the 'Final Solution'* (Cambridge, MA: Harvard University Press, 2002), 155–170. The question of uniqueness has occasioned debates that have generated more heat than light on all sides. The complex history of this debate has been helpfully rehearsed in Gavriel Rosenfeld, 'The Politics of Uniqueness: Reflections on the Recent Polemical Turn in Holocaust and Genocide Scholarship', *Holocaust and Genocide Studies*, 13 (1), 28–61; see also Philip Spencer, 'Un Événement sans Précédent qui crée un Précédent: l'Holocauste et l'Histoire du Génocide', *Bulletin Trimestriel de la Fondation Auschwitz*, 96, 2009: 37–74. It is remarkable that in all these variants of scepticism, collective memory of the Holocaust is treated as a marker of exclusivity serving political purposes antagonistic to the universalistic aspirations of the modern age.

46 See for example http://hmd.org.uk/page/about-hmd-and-hmdt#sthash.Xnl1eqCu .dpuf. For examples of solidarity between survivors, see Union des Étudiants Juifs de France (eds.), *Rwanda: Pour un Dialogue des Memoires* (Paris: Albion Michel, 2007). Ed Vulliamy, who did much to publicise the crimes against humanity committed against Muslims in Bosnia, recounts a speech he heard at a Holocaust conference in

Washington 1998, organised to mark the 50th anniversary of the UN adoption of the Genocide Convention. It was delivered by a man who survived the ghetto liquidation at Kielce, the death camp at Auschwitz and two death marches: 'How do we explain to our children and grandchildren that in the world in which we live ... we diddle and daddle when it comes to mounting a rapid response to save people from destruction from a murderous regime? Oh, I know all the answers we give. They justify our inaction, and the lies we have conditioned ourselves into believing. But the children will see them for what they are, at least as long as they remain children, and retain their empathy for the suffering of others'. This is hardly the stuff of narrow particularism! Ed Vulliamy, *The War is Dead, Long Live the War: Bosnia the Reckoning* (London: Bodley Head, 2012), 72.

47 For evidence that in Italy and Britain those who made the demand to replace Holocaust Memorial Day with Genocide Day have sometimes strayed into antisemitism, see Philip Spencer and Sara Valentina di Palma, 'Antisemitism and the Politics of Holocaust Memorial Day' in Gunther Jikeli and Joelle Allouche-Benayoun (eds.), *Perceptions of the Holocaust in Europe and Muslim Communities* (Heidelberg: Springer 2013), 71–83.

48 See Omer Bartov, *Erased: Vanishing Traces of Jewish Galicia in Present day Ukraine* (New Jersey: Princeton University Press, 2007). For a comprehensive set of essays on the continuing suppression of memory of the murder of Jews see John-Paul Humka and Joanna Beata Miclic (eds.), *Bringing the Dark Past to Light: The Reception of the Holocaust in Eastern Europe* (Lincoln: University of Nebraska Press, 2013). Omer Bartov points out in the final essay that accusations of Zionist instrumentalisation of the Holocaust have had a continuous presence from Communism to post-Communism. See 683–684.

49 Raymond Aron, *Paix et Guerre Entre les Nations* (Paris: Calmann-Levy, 1969), 87–88 (my translation).

50 Ted Honderich, *After the Terror* (Edinburgh: Edinburgh University Press, 2003).

51 Jürgen Habermas, 'A Shirtsleeves Tract: Why I Recommended this Book', www.ucl.ac.uk/~uctytho/BrumlikHabermastrans.html (accessed 28 October 2010), 2004.

52 Habermas, 'A Shirtsleeves Tract'.

6

The return of the Jewish question and the double life of Israel

So now the Jew is mistrusted not for what he is, but for the anti-Semitism of which he is the cause. And no Jew is more the *cause* of anti-Semitism than the Jew who *speaks* of anti-Semitism. (Howard Jacobson, *When Will the Jews be Forgiven for the Holocaust?*)[1]

Those who have always felt that Jews were powerful, controlling and out to destroy the world can now point in the direction of the Middle East and say: there you are. But for the conspiracy theorists, even the most appalling political and military machinations of Binyamin Netanyahu and the Israel Defence Forces – of Israel itself – are far less important than the creation of what David Aaronovitch, *in Voodoo Histories*, describes as a new kind of super-Jew: the Zionist. This is not, for the conspiracy theorist, the straightforward hate figure of the left. Rather, it is a character, or more importantly a group, to which all western governments are secretly in hock: unbelievably rich and powerful, and dedicated unswervingly to its own project, which is nothing less than the complete control of the world. Yes: Zionists are basically Spectre. (David Baddiel, 'Short of a Conspiracy Theory? You Can Always Blame the Jews').[2]

The most significant expression of the reconfiguring of the Jewish question in the present period lies in the rise of negative representations of Israel and Zionism. While the stigmatisation of the idea of a Jewish nation may be traced back to the Enlightenment credo that everything should be granted to Jews 'as individuals' and nothing to Jews 'as a nation', it frames the Jewish question today in ways that could not have existed prior to the actual rise of Zionism as a political movement and especially prior to the formation of the state of Israel after the Holocaust.

It should go without saying that criticism of Israel is no less or more problematic than criticism of any other country.[3] There is of course much to criticise, including occupation of Palestinian land, human rights abuses that flow from the occupation, anti-Arab racism in civil society, discriminatory state policies toward Israeli Palestinians, militaristic responses to external threats, etc. Nor does it exonerate the *singularity* of harms done by Israel to argue that the policies of neighbouring states are equally or in some cases far more subject to political criticism. The fact that other states do not live up to their responsibilities does not release Israel from its responsibilities for equal treatment of its citizens, for solidarity with strangers, for actively seeking an end to occupation, and for combating racism of all kinds. Criticism of Israel for its 'identitarian' constitutional status as a *Jewish* state is not invalidated by the fact that many of the states in the Middle East and North Africa analogously define themselves as 'Arab' or 'Islamic'. It is a predicament of all modern nation states to have to deal with contradictions that arise between the universal norms of constitutional government and the national boundaries in which these norms are set. Israel is no exception to this general rule.

It should also go without saying that 'criticism' of any country *can* be racist, antisemitic, Islamophobic or bigoted. We are familiar with the phenomenon of racial stereotypes parading as political criticism. When in response to injustices perpetrated by states or social movements we hear pseudo-anthropological statements concerning whole categories of people – for example, that, Africans cannot rule themselves, Arabs cannot comprehend democracy, Orientals do not value individuality, Americans are crassly materialistic, Europeans are marked by a postcolonial sense of their own superiority, etc. – it should be clear that criticism of *any* country *can* be imbued with prejudice. Witness the lengths to which citizens of postcolonial states go to distinguish *democratic* criticism of their own political regimes from negative stereotypes of 'peoples' that come from without. What is called 'criticism' of Israel is no exception. It may be based on the Jewishness of the people rather than on the democratic shortcomings of the state, or on some fusion of both. It may be premised on the harmfulness attributed to the idea of a 'Jewish nation' as such. Antisemitic criticism of Israel has parallels with racist criticism of other countries.

The problem we reference, that of viewing 'Israel' and 'Zionism' through the lens of the Jewish question, has much in common with the criminalisation of individuals. The criminalisation process has been explored within the discipline of sociology and the sub-discipline of the sociology of deviance. It involves both mechanisms of selection, interpretation, individuation and projection as well as incarceration, isolation, discipline and punishment.[4] While the criminalisation of individuals on the one hand and that of states and peoples on the other are not identical processes, they share commonalities worth exploring. They include tendencies to essentialise the subject as fundamentally deviant; to single out only those actions of the subject that are indicative of wrongdoing; to interpret actions of the subject through an accusatory lens; to represent the subject only in relation to the question of guilt; to abstract the actions of the subject from their inter-subjective and interactive contexts; to evaluate the subject in terms of deviation from abstract ideals no one can live up to; to project onto the subject the wrongs that exist in ourselves; and to bifurcate the world into two camps of criminality and honest society. Analogy between criminalising processes and the criminalisation of a whole people, nation or state is intended to help us think about what is involved in seeing Israel and Zionism through the lens of the Jewish question. We can illustrate the problem by exploring further the guilty verdicts passed on Israel and Zionism in some current 'critical' discourses.

Perhaps the most shocking of these is the charge of genocide, where Israel is accused of the very crime whose commission against Jews made the necessity for such a state so compelling. It forms part of the charge that Israel acts toward Palestinians 'like' Nazis acted toward Jews.[5] As defined in the Genocide Convention of 1948, the crime of genocide specifies that it must involve intent to destroy a group in whole or in part through a series of actions of which mass killing is key but which also include causing serious bodily and mental harm, deliberately inflicting conditions of life calculated to bring about the physical destruction of the group, imposing measures intended to prevent births in the targeted group or forcibly transferring children of the targeted group to another group. There has been debate over such clauses. For example, after much legal argument, the International Tribunal on the Genocide in Rwanda came to the view that intent on the part of the perpetrator was a necessary component of a successful charge but could be deduced from foreseeable consequences and outcomes alone.[6] To justify a charge of genocide in the case of the state of Israel, one would have to evidence the application of these criteria to Israel's treatment of Palestinians. It would have to be shown, for instance, that the Palestinian people have been destroyed as a group in part or whole and that the state of Israel has shown intent to commit genocide through measures designed to expel Palestinians, prevent Palestinian births, transfer Palestinian children to Israeli families, destroy Palestinian culture, etc.[7] In relation to the conflict that took place during the Gaza war of 2014, in which over 2000 Palestinian soldiers and civilians were killed, as well as over 70 Israelis, it would have to be shown not only that physical destruction involving serious war crimes was committed by both sides but that the crimes committed by Israeli forces constituted genocide, which is by its nature a one-sided crime. Some insight may be gained by comparing charges of genocide directed against Israel in the course of the Gaza war with their relative absence when the Assad regime in Syria, only a few miles to the north, was responsible in the same period for killing well over 200,000 Syrians including some 2,400 Palestinians.

The charge of genocide does not bear close analytical scrutiny. It is not the result of informed political judgment of the kind upon which Hannah Arendt was so insistent, which requires us to think for ourselves, directly and carefully, about the application of concepts to particulars, to make meaningful comparisons, and to use appropriate standards of judgment to distinguish between crimes of a different order and magnitude.[8] This failure indicates how what at first appears as a major sign of progress can be turned into its opposite.

Humanitarian law is a case in point. Today it has rightly become part of the formal structure of international law. It not only claims a 'soft' influence over states to take human rights into account but, in some instances, to demand compliance and declare a duty to obey. The norms of international law function as a higher law vis-à-vis that of states and there is an increasing number of treaty-based norms that obligate all states, whether or not they have signed the treaty in question. These include prohibition on genocide, as well as crimes against humanity, disappearances and torture. The dependence of international law on state consent has declined, as has the state's degree of freedom in interpreting and enforcing international law. International law is no longer involved only in conflicts *between* states but also in conflicts *within* states, affording international law a bigger role in responding to events such as civil wars, human rights abuses and humanitarian crimes.

One of the offshoots of the expanded scope of international law is the expanded use of categories of humanitarian law in political argument. Whether an act on the part of a state or state-supported actors is deemed to be in violation of international humanitarian law is now advanced as a basis for deciding on the legitimacy of the act in question and in some cases of the actor. Human rights have become the stuff of public debate, especially since the end of the Cold War, and their present public status contrasts with their relative invisibility in the post-1945 period, when international law was widely regarded as ineffective or narrowly technocratic in its concerns, and when citizens were inclined to rely on the resources of domestic legal systems or on their own moral and political judgments unmediated by law. The authority of humanitarian and human rights law has been invoked from a surprising number of intellectual and political perspectives, including critical-legal perspectives that do not normally uphold positive law as a privileged standard of legitimacy. It is difficult to imagine political argument any longer doing without this normative resource. Both the terminology of humanitarian law (not only genocide but also crimes of aggression, war crimes, crimes against humanity, torture, disproportionate response, collective punishment, etc.) and the terminology of human rights law (inhuman and degrading treatment, right to life, right to family life, right to free expression, etc.) play a vital role in public debate, as well as in legal judgment and this is as it should be. Were we to abandon this resource and revert back to a form of political argument in which notions of national interest on the one hand and moral claims of imperial powers on the other were the only prevailing points of reference, a vital ingredient of political argument that ties it to ethical life would certainly be lost.

The appeal to human rights in political argument, however, has a down side that disturbs this sense of progress. First, appeal may be made not to what humanitarian and human rights norms *actually are* but to some notion of what they *ought to be* or to the *values* they are supposed to embody, even when these values require the reform of actually existing international laws for their realisation. Second, the claim that an act of state accords with or violates humanitarian or human rights law is rarely tested in a judicial court, more often in the court of public opinion, and in political argument claims typically rely on the opinions of politicians and academics. The checks and balances that surround the expression of judicial opinion in legal cases are generally absent in political argument, so that the opinions expressed all too often utilise a selective interpretation of international law to support already pre-determined particular political convictions. Third, the appeal to one or other category of humanitarian or human rights law in political argument may be based not on the legal definition of the category in question, in this case on what is legally meant by 'genocide', but on common usage that may substantially differ from legal definitions. These categories are used in order to give rhetorical weight to an argument, whether or not there is an actual relation between what is claimed to be morally right and what is legally right according to the norms of international law. Fourth, humanitarian and human rights law form a complex array of norms, and different parties tend to pick and choose those aspects that favour their interests or convictions. One side may be well disposed to those elements of international law that outlaw terrorism but not those that relate to the mistreatment of prisoners of war. Another side may be better disposed to those elements of international law that uphold a right of resistance against occupation but less keen on international law's injunctions against harming civilians. Finally, both parties may be disdainful of existing norms of humanitarian law on the grounds that they are controlled by their opponents, but still use the rhetoric of humanitarianism and human rights to accuse the other of hypocrisy.[9]

These tendencies may be illustrated by debates in the *Guardian* newspaper in the UK over the legality as well as legitimacy of the Israeli invasion of Gaza in January 2009. One letter to the *Guardian* runs: 'As international lawyers, we remind the UK government that it has a duty under international law to exert its influence to stop violations of international humanitarian law in the current conflict between Israel and Hamas. A fundamental principle of international humanitarian law is that the parties to a conflict must distinguish between civilians and those who participate directly in hostilities' (14 January, 2009). This even-handed approach to the distinction between civilians and combatants was matched by numerous attempts to place international law on one side or the other of the conflict. The British Committee for the Universities of Palestine wrote in their Declaration of 'Gaza's Guernica': 'We say enough is enough. As long as the state of Israel continues to defy humanity and international law, we, the citizens of the world, commit ourselves to boycotting Israel' (28 December, 2008). On the other side, in response to the UNHCR Report on Gaza, one respondent argued that 'Hamas knowingly and deliberately targeted civilians and civilian targets in Israel and based itself in civilian areas' whilst there was no evidence that the phosphorous shells Israel used in civilian areas had been used 'in an illegal way' (7 May, 2009). When we look more closely at the appeal to humanitarian law in political argument, we find a propensity for all that is solid to melt into air.

Treating categories of humanitarian law, such as genocide, as trump cards that function to conclude argument saves us the work of having to make our own case. While such categories have rightly become a necessary part of political argument, they can all too easily substitute for political argument. To turn them into an absolute standard against which to measure the actions of states is to open a space for instrumentalising human rights, and paradoxically for undermining the basis of their own legitimacy.[10] The application of concepts to particulars should be a matter of reflective judgment and not merely of instrumental utility.

A second charge has to do with the so-called 'apartheid analogy'. Here an analogy is drawn between Israel and the racist regime in South Africa, which at the tail end of the colonial era was rightly seen as a wholly illegitimate form of state. Certain aspects of what Israel has become, notably its occupation of Palestine and its colonial-like domination of Palestinians who live in Palestinian territory, have been converted into the central meaning of what Israel is. Contingent similarities between what Israel has become and the former apartheid state of South Africa have been translated into an essential identity. Certain contiguities between Israel and apartheid have thus shaded into what we call the 'apartheid analogy', and the chain of equivalence linking Israel and apartheid has come to form a standard trope in a diversity of left political circles. In classic antisemitism, 'the Jew' was treated as the symbolic representation of all that is rotten in the modern world. In contemporary antizionism we see a related phenomenon: Israel, Zionism and the Jewish state are treated as symbolic representations of all that is illegitimate in the present-day international community. Apartheid was the name of an overtly racist regime that deserved the opprobrium and isolation it received. In the metonymic use of apartheid, however, Israel is not called by its own name or understood in its own right but through the name of something seemingly associated with it. This rhetorical device has in turn been converted through processes of slippage into the metaphoric use of 'apartheid' in order to designate the core being of Israel. The attempt to portray an equivalence between Israel and apartheid has been pursued through a synecdoche in which the part – say the shooting of Palestinian demonstrators by Israeli soldiers or attacks on ordinary Palestinian civilians by Israeli settlers – is taken for the whole and then analogised with apartheid. In these ideologically charged slippages from contingency to essence, from metonymy to metaphor, from part to the whole, from contiguity to analogy, the missing term is that of comparison.

To simply say that the 'Jewish state' is like apartheid, or is apartheid, is no substitute for analysis that studies similarities and differences between the one and the other. We might compare, for instance, gender inequalities in Saudi Arabia with racial inequalities under apartheid, or the constitution of the 'Jewish' state with that of 'Arab' or 'Islamic' states, or both with allegedly 'cosmopolitan' states in Europe. Analogy, however, saves us the work of comparison. We might also compare struggles against apartheid in South Africa – which found expression in documents like the Freedom Charter and were generally conducted in the name of achieving democracy – with struggles in Israel-Palestine, which have found expression in documents like the Hamas Covenant and Hezbollah Manifesto (which appear to provide no place for Jewish nationhood in 'Muslim' lands and scarcely more space for individual Jews). In place of comparison, a method of choice is to contrast the existing state of Israel to an abstract idea of what the state ought to be and then decree that it falls short. According to this rhetoric, the state ought to be cosmopolitan, universalistic, emptied of identitarian content, but the 'Jewish democratic state' of Israel violates this idea; or nationalism ought to be civic without any ethnic content but Zionism obstructs the realisation of this contemporary ideal. A more comparative method would compare how the 'Jewish democratic state' of Israel deals with the contradictory demands of state and nation with how other states deal with their own contradictory demands. The functional equivalence between such representations of Israel and apartheid lies in their power of delegitimation. Unable to create any genuine links, this rhetoric ends up with a form of catachresis that substitutes one term for the other. It means that Israel is not called by its own name but by the name of something else that was by common consent fit only for abolition.[11]

A third charge is that Israel is a major threat to world peace. This may be illustrated by a debate conducted in 2012 around a poem published by the celebrated German novelist Günter Grass, '*Was Gesagt Werden Muß*' ('What Must Be Said').[12] Christine Achinger recounts that most German critics did not claim the poem was antisemitic but criticised Grass for maintaining that Israel was threatening a nuclear attack on Iran that would 'extinguish the Iranian people', that Israel was a threat to world peace while President Ahmadinejad of Iran was merely a 'loud mouth', and that the threat of an Iranian nuclear bomb was a 'mere legend'. Grass was also criticised for claiming to break the silence imposed by the threat of being called antisemitic, while he had only recently broken his own silence about having been drafted by the Nazi regime as a member of the Waffen-SS. Achinger shows that German newspapers were generally critical of the Netanyahu government and warned against an Israeli attack on Iranian nuclear installations, but the main point for Grass' critics was that he presented Israelis as the new Nazis and Germans as cowed into silence by Israeli power. The characteristically ham-fisted reaction of the Netanyahu government, to bar Grass from entering Israel, lent superficial plausibility to Grass' self-presentation.

A rush of readers' comments in German and British newspapers alleged that Grass was being hounded as a supposed 'antisemite' for no other reason than that he had dared criticise Israel. A translation of the poem published in the *Guardian* on 5 April 2012 reduced it to less than half its original length and omitted without any indication the most problematic passages. This made it harder for an English-language reader to see the German debate as anything other than a knee-jerk reaction to criticism of Israel. In a demagogic response, the Marxist writer Tariq Ali dispensed with any reference to the actual debate when he condemned the 'disgusting attacks on Gunter Grass'. According to Ali, Zionist self-assertion that 'the crime against the Jews of Europe was unique in the annals of history' combined with Zionist control over the media and American foreign policy to prevent ordinary people from recognising the crimes of Israel. The view that Grass' poem was labelled antisemitic in order to immunise Israel against criticism does no justice to a debate that had more to do with Europe's relation to its past than with Israel and Palestine. The expression of concern over antisemitism was treated as a sign of Zionist power and cunning rather than as the expression of a critical consciousness keen to avoid conspiracy theories in understanding modern society.[13]

The three charges against Israel and Zionism we have briefly discussed – genocide, apartheid and threat to world peace – bear little analytical scrutiny, but the mark of the Jewish question is to elide suspicion with guilt. It represents Israel as the worst form of state, the Jewish nation as the worst sort of nationalism, and Jews who identify with Israel or refuse to condemn it as the worst accomplices. The rhetorical function of these charges is to say that there can be no greater crimes than those committed by Israel and its supporters; that Israel is the embodiment of criminality or evil, and that it must be punished through exclusion from the society of peoples. That the criminalisation of Israel also involves coercive measures we can illustrate here through two examples: the UK academic boycott campaign and the *Charlie Hebdo* affair in Paris.

The gravity of the charges made against Israel and Zionism have provided some of the emotional force behind the move to boycott Israeli academe, which has now become part of a larger campaign for Boycott, Disinvestment and Sanctions. In turn the boycott campaign has sustained the gravity of these charges in order to justify its own practices. As Pascal put it, if first you kneel, then you will believe.[14] There is nothing new in the deployment of boycotts as a weapon of struggle. Consumer boycotts were deployed in apartheid South Africa by independent non-racial unions to put pressure on employers to meet workers' needs and trade union demands. At the other end of the legitimacy scale antisemitic boycotts were used by the National Socialists in Germany to exclude Jews from the social and economic life of the country. The academic boycott of which we now speak is aimed at singling out Israeli academic institutions, and only *Israeli* academic institutions, from the global academic community.

The early history of this boycott campaign within academic unions in the UK goes back to the 1980s when some left groups labelled Israel 'the illegitimate state' and called for the 'no-platforming' of 'Zionist' organisations on university campuses. This campaign effectively singled out some Jewish Societies that had previously participated in the antiracist Anti-Nazi League. Some left-wing groups, who originally lent support to the campaign in a misplaced show of solidarity with the Palestinian struggle, backed off when confronted with basic antiracist arguments.[15] When the boycott campaign resumed some fifteen years later, the climate had markedly deteriorated. In 2004 the Association of University Teachers (AUT) passed a motion which deplored the alleged 'witch-hunting' of colleagues who supported academic boycott of Israel, affirmed categorically that 'anti-Zionism is not anti-Semitism', and resolved to give support to members 'unjustly accused of anti-Semitism because of their political opposition to Israeli government policy'. In 2005 the AUT council resolved to boycott two Israeli universities, Haifa and Bar Ilan; when the vote was contested and a special meeting of the union convened, the boycott proposal was rejected. The successor union, University and College Union passed repeated resolutions calling for the boycott of Israeli academic institutions and repudiating any antisemitic connotation. In 2006 a resolution was passed denying that 'criticism of the Israeli government is *in itself* anti-Semitic' (our emphasis) and claiming that 'defenders of the Israeli government's actions have used a charge of anti-Semitism as a tactic in order to smother democratic debate and in the context of Higher Education to restrict academic freedom'. At the 2007 congress it was resolved that 'criticism of Israel *cannot* be construed as anti-Semitic' and at the 2008 congress that 'criticisms of Israel or Israeli policy are not, *as such*, anti-Semitic' (our emphasis). When complaints were made of the union's discrimination against opponents of the boycott campaign, of its invitation to pro-boycott speakers with proven antisemitic records, and of its indifference to concerns about antisemitism expressed by members, they were unanswered or rejected. In 2011 the union voted to dissociate itself from what was at the time a 'working definition of antisemitism' adopted by the European Union Monitoring Commission. Its most contentious clause focused on attempts to draw some kind of line between legitimate political criticism of Israel and antisemitic stigmatisation. The union maintained that the 'working definition' enabled opponents of the boycott to cry 'antisemitism' to stop people taking peaceful action against Israel, but had nothing to say about proponents of the boycott crying 'Israel' to stop people taking action against antisemitism. The cumulative effect of these initiatives was to remove antisemitism from the array of racisms the union would address if and when some kind of connection could be made with 'criticism of Israel'.

The key questions that challenged the academic boycott included the following: why is Israel being singled out for boycott when other countries are as or more repressive; why are Israeli civil society institutions sanctioned for crimes allegedly committed by the Israeli state; why is the exclusion of Israeli academic institutions from the global academic community not discriminatory on the basis of nationality or on the basis of religion if only Jewish members are targeted; why is the legal fiction endorsed that academic institutions can be boycotted without affecting the academic freedom of their members; why are normal procedures of solidarity with fellow trade unionists and academics not being followed in this case? And why are the key principles which the union supports – academic freedom, freedom of speech, exchange of ideas, rational argumentation, access to voices with which one might disagree, etc. – suspended? Proponents of the academic boycott have provided their own answers but the force of these questions has led them to make ever more wild and hypertrophic characterisations of Israel and Zionism. The academic boycott movement exemplifies the slippage from political criticism of a *state* to condemnation of a *people*. There is no reason to doubt the sincerity of those boycotters who present themselves as having *no antisemitic* intent, but this does not address their responsibilities regarding the *effects of actions* designed to unite conflicting political forces around the stigmatisation of Israel and *the intent of others* drawn into the campaign.

Some of the dangers we identify here were realised in the case of the murders that took place in Paris in early 2015 when, under the register of *Je suis Charlie*, a demonstration of an estimated million and a half people was held in Paris, and another million and a half people took to the streets elsewhere in France. They were among the largest public demonstrations in French history, held in protest against the murder of ten editors and cartoonists of *Charlie Hebdo*, a left-wing magazine, for having published cartoons representing the prophet Mohammed, one security officer and one (Muslim) police officer for having been in the way, and four shoppers in a Kosher supermarket for having been Jewish. The murders had an explicitly antisemitic dimension: the four Jews killed in the kosher supermarket were killed because they were Jews; the one woman on the editorial board of *Charlie Hebdo* who was murdered seems to have been murdered because she was Jewish. The murder of these Jews in Paris followed the murders of four people in the Jewish Museum in Brussels and before that of a parent and three schoolchildren (two of them his own) in a Jewish school in Toulouse.[16] It was followed by the murder of a Jewish security guard outside a synagogue in Copenhagen. The murderers themselves were supporters of a jihadi Islamist movement, Al Qaeda in Yemen, which wore its antisemitism openly on its sleeve. The mass demonstrations against the killings expressed popular support for freedom of expression, religious tolerance, and opposition to religious fundamentalism. As one commentator put it, they represented resistance to 'the assassin's veto on critical discourse'.[17]

At the same time a discourse developed among left intellectuals that expressed scepticism toward the demonstrations that evolved in some instances into pejorative assessments of the public display of solidarity with the murdered people.[18]

Mehdi Hasan, writing 'as a Muslim', caught this mood when he maintained that *Je suis Charlie* was a symbol of the prejudices of the 'enlightened liberal West against backward barbaric Muslims'. He wrote that it was premised on double standards, since the journal refused cartoons mocking the Holocaust and had sacked one cartoonist (Maurice Sinet) in 2008 for antisemitic cartoons. Hasan maintained that *Charlie Hebdo* affirmed a right to offend Muslims without any corresponding notion of responsibility, assumed Muslims should have thicker skins, and used racist imagery to attack members of a powerless minority religion. He maintained that the solidarity demonstration was premised on the illusion of untrammelled freedom of speech and the hypocrisy of Western leaders supporting freedom of speech when, as he put it, Obama was demanding that Yemen jail an anti-drone journalist and Merkel was supporting laws against Holocaust denial. He also wrote that it 'sickened' him to see Benjamin Netanyahu, the right-wing Prime Minister of Israel, at the demonstration.[19]

There is a problem of double standards when national leaders link arms in defence of freedom of expression, which some violently suppress in their own countries. It is arguable whether a hypocritical show of commitment to freedom of expression is better than no show at all, but the existence of double standards *within the elite* underlines the significance of people defending this freedom consistently and protesting when it is violated. Those, for example, who oppose bans on the headscarf and burqa in French public institutions on freedom of religion grounds, would as a matter of sheer consistency be expected to defend *Charlie Hebdo* and oppose laws that criminalise blasphemy and apostasy. The cartoonist Bernard Holtrop commented on their newfound friends in the elite with characteristic *Charlie Hebdo* vigour: 'we vomit on all these people'. The hypocrisy of elites does not make freedom of speech itself any less valuable. The journal's attacks on the idea of 'blasphemy' represented acts of solidarity with secularists in countries that criminalise blasphemy, and are a reminder that the first victims of jihadism are usually Muslims. They are an expression of solidarity with journalists assassinated by Islamic fundamentalist forces (like the Syrian Raed Fares by ISIS) or brutally punished by the Saudi Arabian government (like the blogger Raif Badawi).

The danger of Islamophobic appropriation of the protest by movements like the French *Front National*, and other nationalist forces opposed to the 'Islamicisation of Europe', should not allow us to forget that the assembly of people who gathered in Place de la République overwhelmingly expressed inclusive and democratic rather than Islamophobic sentiments, or that the organisers of the demonstration explicitly excluded the *Front National*. The representation of *Charlie Hebdo* as Islamophobic has been deployed as grounds for withdrawing solidarity from the victims of the violence. There is, however, an obvious difference between defending someone's right to say something, including something controversial and shocking, and endorsing the content of what is said. The critique of the content of the cartoons as Islamophobic is in any event highly tendentious. The ambiguities of Luiz's cartoon of the prophet Muhammad shedding a tear under the words *Tout est pardonné* and carrying a placard saying *Je suis Charlie* are part of its strength, but the cartoon suggests that Muhammad, whose name was invoked by nihilistic men of violence, is innocent of the crimes they committed. An earlier cartoon has Muhammad in tears saying: *c'est dur d'etre aimé par des cons* ('it's hard being loved by shits'); another has Muhammad beheaded by a black masked fanatic under the words 'If Muhammad returned'; and a third has a cartoonist in gay embrace with a bearded Mullah under the words *L'amour plus fort que la haine* ('Love stronger than hate'), which became one of the slogans of the demonstrations. The point is not to defend everything *Charlie Hebdo* did, but its attacks on 'religious' targets of different denominations go back to a Rabelaisian and then revolutionary anti-clerical tradition. There was a cartoon of Catholic priests declaring that 'every sperm is sacred' and another of an Israeli Jewish settler killing a Palestinian farmer and saying 'Take that, Goliath'. *Charlie Hebdo* was a creature of the post-68 New Left, remained on the left and had close ties with *SOS Racisme*. The editor Charb was in the *Front de Gauche*, campaigned against neoliberal changes to the European constitution, and illustrated *Marx: A User's Guide*. Bernard Maris, a co-editor, was a member of an anti-globalisation movement called *Attac* and campaigned against austerity, corporate corruption, tax havens and the arms industry. Being on the left does not mean that one is not Islamophobic but the damaging attacks that have been launched on the journal bring to mind similar attacks on the work of Salman Rushdie after a Fatwa was declared against him in 1989.[20]

In this *Alice in Wonderland* world, everything is upside down. Reaction in the form of jihadi dreams of a Caliphate, conspiracy thinking about Jews undermining Islam, and attacks on Muslims who disagree, is treated as counter-hegemonic, while antiracism and anti-homophobia in the form of *Charlie Hebdo* are treated as reaction. The most important distinctions are not made: like that between speech designed to incite violence and hatred which is not and should not be protected in law, and speech that is anti-religious and may appear blasphemous from the point of view of the pious, which is and should be protected.[21] The prosecution of the comedian Dieudonné M'bala M'bala for inciting hatred of Jews (after he declared *inter alia* 'Je suis Charlie Coulibaly', the name of the killer of Jews in the supermarket), may be likened to that of the actor Brigitte Bardot and journalist Eric Zemmour for inciting hatred of Muslims; they were all designed to protect people from violence. Laws against blasphemy by contrast protect the state and state-endorsed religions from the people.

As far as the antisemitic dimensions of the violence were concerned, one response has been to neglect it altogether or draw some kind of equivalence between the killing of French Jews in Paris and the killing of Palestinians in Israel. In a competition of victimhood in which concern for one supplants concern for the other, the notion is born that injustices committed by 'Jews' could go some way toward explaining the rage that led to 'their' murder.[22] Rather than see Islamophobia and antisemitism as connected forms of racism, the temptation is to set up what Kenan Malik calls an 'auction of victimhood' in which 'every group attempts to outbid all others as the one feeling most offended'.[23] Let us not lose sight of the *connection* between the attack on *Charlie Hebdo* and that on Jews – that the attack was simultaneously directed at the right to freedom of expression *and* at the lives of Jews. Even if the grocery shoppers were innocent, it has been said, it is a reminder that Jews a thousand miles away are guilty of terrible crimes against Islam.[24] But let us not confound the pretext given for crimes and our understanding of them. In Toulouse the pretext given by Mohammed Mera for killing Jews was that 'the Jews kill our brothers and sisters in Palestine'. In the *Charlie Hebdo* affair, the pretext given by the Kouachi brothers was to 'avenge the Prophet Muhammad'. In the random killing of 130 people on 13 November 2015 in Paris, the pretext given by the Islamic State of Iraq and the Levant (ISIL), which claimed responsibility for the attacks, was that they were in retaliation for French airstrikes on ISIL targets in Syria and Iraq.[25] Pretexts are significant but it would be erroneous to treat the killers as spokespeople of the wider Muslim community or conclude that if only the Israelis had not killed Muslims in Palestine, if only *Charlie Hebdo* had not caused offence with its cartoons, if only the French air force had not bombed targets in Syria and Iraq, then the *raison d'être* of the attacks would no longer exist.

The return of the Jewish question

Contempt for rights, lack of solidarity with victims, neglect of antisemitism, belief in the harmfulness of Jews – the markers of the old Jewish question are not absent in the new. The practical problem is how to transcend this whole perspective. At issue is our capacity to smell the scent and hear the echoes of an old prejudice even when it assumes the forms of enlightenment, progressiveness, antiracism and cosmopolitanism. The point is not to abandon these principles but to stay with their substance. Sometimes we have to rely on our own judgment even if it is at odds with the opinion of many good people around us. If the markers of our cosmopolitan existence are indeed a common sense in which we learn to share a common world with others, and an enlarged mentality in which we learn to see the world from the standpoint of others,[26] these are the very capacities the Jewish question excises when it demands that consciousness of sharing a common world with Israel, and seeing the world from its standpoints, should in principle be renounced.

The return of the Jewish question involves a distortion of universalism that sees Jews as *the* problem and demands a solution to this problem. Today this demand focuses on the exclusion of the Jewish nation from world society.

Condemning a people is no substitute for political thought, even if it presents itself as resistance to power, speaks the language of universalism and prides itself on its left credentials.[27] The practical question for the left is how to escape the prison house of the Jewish question.

The Jewish question is not just an attitude of hostility to Jews or to those who invoke the sign of 'the Jews' but a theory designed to explain the winners and losers of capitalist society. It is formulated in terms of dichotomies – the modern and the backward, the people and its enemies, the civic and the ethnic, the postnational and the national, imperialism and anti-imperialism, power and resistance, the West and the rest. In every case Jews appear as the 'other of the universal': a backward people who stubbornly resist progress or an all-too-clever people who manipulate progress and hold the world in its thrall; a nation within a nation that is endemically treacherous or a nation unlike all other nations in that it is not a valid nation at all; a 'settler-colonial' state in an otherwise decolonised world or a 'cosmopolitan elite' with no comprehension of global responsibility.[28] The 'othering' of Jews inevitably creates an inequitable economy of compassion and a restrictive arena of solidarity.[29] In its spiritless radicalism it at once turns Israel into the primary source of violence in the world and places Palestinians into a single identity script as victims, only as victims and only as victims of Israel. Just as it subsumes the plurality of Jewish voices to 'the Jews' and the plurality of Israeli voices to 'Israel', it also subsumes the plurality of Palestinian voices to 'the Palestinians' and risks turning them into ciphers of our own resentments. It erases uncertainty and complexity in favour of a bifurcated economy of identity and non-identity. It makes us blind to the universal insight that no human being is entirely different from another even where unequal social structures and cultural peculiarities make this hard to see.[30] Israel is represented not as a complex society with real people embroiled in internal and external conflicts, but as a vessel into which 'we' who cannot shake off the illusion of our own universality – be it we Europeans, we on the left, we cosmopolitans, or we diasporic Jews – project what is most troubling in ourselves and so preserve the good for ourselves. Jews never were the problem; they are not the problem now. What has to be dealt with is not a Jewish question, but the question of antisemitism that generated the Jewish question in the first place.

A first step toward emancipating the left from the shadow of the Jewish question is to recognise what it is: not only in its emphatically antisemitic form as 'the final solution' but also in its less lethal forms *within* Enlightenment, *within* emancipation struggles, *within* revolutionary Marxism, *within* critical theories, *within* solidarity movements, and *within* the contemporary left. While classic antisemitism constitutes the bottom line of the Jewish question, in all its forms it is premised on projections concerning the harmfulness of Jews that has a deep affinity to antisemitism. Today there are not many who raise the spectre of the Jewish question as an explicit question to be set and solved, but if it has mainly gone underground it does not mean that it no longer exists. It still provides the grammar, vocabulary, theoretical premises – in short, the conceptual ground – on which antisemitism can continue to grow. The Jewish question is a discourse of prejudice toward Jews, but it is also a discourse of ignorance and obfuscation that distorts our understanding of the world and our conception of humanity. The posing of this question inflicts harm on all who pose it. When the left succumbs, we should not be surprised if the result is not only to disable it from providing solidarity to Jews even when they are most under attack, but also to fail at a general level to recognise that all human beings are members of a common humanity and that our human status matters whatever particular category we belong to. The good news is that in the struggle to supersede the Jewish question we do not start from scratch. In fact, we have the best traditions of critical thought to inspire and guide us.

Notes

1 Howard Jacobson, *When Will the Jews be Forgiven for the Holocaust?*

2 David Baddiel, 'Short of a Conspiracy Theory? You Can Always Blame the Jews', *Guardian*, 22 July 2015.

3 It is difficult to say anything about Israel itself that does not provoke ideologically driven responses. Suffice to say that in Israel we find a state that was brought into being in reaction to the near-destruction of those designated Jews, authorised by the international community through the United Nations, confronted by the hostility of other newly independent states which defined themselves as 'Arab' and which denied the legitimacy of a 'Jewish' state. Its population was swollen by surviving European Jews who could find no place in the West and by 'Arab Jews' expelled or excluded from newly independent states in the Middle East and Maghreb. Neighbouring Arab states did not accept the UN division of the British mandate of Palestine into two states and sought to conquer and divide the territory between themselves. In the course of wars with these states, Israel was implicated in driving out or not allowing back in a substantial part of the Arab population of Palestine and in discriminatory practices against the substantial Palestinian minority that remained in Israel. A complex and an original array of elements came together in the formation of Israel, which only look like the unfolding of the original idea of Zionism in retrospect. The unacceptable occupation of Palestine since 1967 has been one result of these unending hostilities. No understanding of Israel can flow from already possessed truths, or from a conception of 'Zionism' as an evolving essence, or from imposed silences. Our understanding is bound to be distorted if we proceed as if the Holocaust never happened, as if Jews were not forced out of 'Arab' lands, as if Israel were never attacked, as if Jewish national movements do not have commonalities with other national movements, as if there is no plurality in Israeli society, and as if violence does not have intersubjective origins.

4 For our own elaboration of the criminalisation thesis, see Robert Fine, 'Labelling Theory: An Investigation into the Sociological Critique of Deviance', *Economy and*

Society, 6 (2), 1977: 166–193; 'Bourgeois Power: Sartre and the Modern Prison', *Economy and Society*, 6 (4), 1977: 408–435; and 'Struggles against Discipline: The Theory and Politics of Michel Foucault' in Barry Smart (ed.), *Michel Foucault: Critical Assessments* (London: Routledge, 1994).

5 There are more or less sophisticated versions of this charge. For examples of the cruder kind, see those cited in Spencer and Valentina di Palma, 'Antisemitism and the Politics of Holocaust Memorial day in the UK and Italy', 71–83. More sophisticated charges have been mounted by, for example, Martin Shaw in 'The Question of Genocide in Palestine in 1948', and rebutted by Omer Bartov in 'The Question of Genocide in Palestine in 1948: A Reply to Martin Shaw', both in *Journal of Genocide Research*, 12 (3 and 4), 243–259.

6 Issues concerning the definition of genocide are discussed in Philip Spencer, *Genocide since 1945* (London: Routledge, 2012), 13–14.

7 The 'genocide' thesis in relation to Israel is discussed in Philip Spencer, 'The Left, Radical Antisemitism, and the Problem of Genocide', *Journal for the Study of Antisemitism*, 2 (2010), 501–519.

8 In this context, it is striking how those who claim to follow Hannah Arendt in attacking Israel seem to have entirely ignored her own writings on what is in involved in political judgment.

9 A case in point is the contention that international criminal courts are selective in whom they choose to prosecute for war crimes, a selectivity based not on the nature of the crimes that have been committed or on the harm they have caused but on who the accused are and whether they are deemed allies or enemies of those who authorise the court. This argument has been raised to question the legitimacy of existing international criminal courts and tribunals (David Chandler, 'International Justice' in Daniele Archibugi (ed.), *Debating Cosmopolitics* (London: Verso, 2003), 27–39). However, the fact that some offenders are not prosecuted does not invalidate the prosecution of others in this sphere of law, any more than the fact that some speeding offences are not prosecuted does not invalidate the prosecution of others.

10 Our observations concerning the expanded scope of international humanitarian law in political argument are drawn from Robert Fine, 'Thoughts on the Legitimacy of Human Rights' in Aldo Mascareno and Kathya Araujo (eds.), *Legitimization in World Society* (Farnham: Ashgate 2012), 25–44.

11 The same kind of problem is present in the idea that Israel is a 'settler-colonial' state. This label requires serious analysis but comes from applying a pre-existing model of states colonised by European powers to a situation with its own distinctive characteristics. Many of the 'colonisers' did not come from 'the West' but from Eastern Europe and Arab lands; they were normally fleeing persecution which became genocidal in Europe; they perceived an attachment to this particular area that was born in part out of the fact that Jews had lived there for millennia; and they entered a world of competing national movements (Zionist, Arab nationalist, Palestinian, Islamist, etc.) which developed in the same post-imperial space. The danger present in the use of this negative epithet is that rather than stimulate thought and judgment, it substitutes for them.

12　We are indebted to the research of the German scholar Christine Achinger for this analysis. See Christine Achinger and Robert Fine, 'Introduction' in Christine Achinger and Robert Fine (eds.), *Antisemitism, Racism and Islamophobia: Distorted Faces of Modernity* (London: Routledge, 2015), 1–13.

13　Tariq Ali, 'The Disgusting Attacks on Gunter Grass', *Counterpunch*, 10 April 2012, www.counterpunch.org/2012/04/10/the-disgusting-attacks-on-gunter-grass/ (accessed 10 September 2014).

14　Slavoj Žižek analyses the dialectic of kneeling and believing thus: 'Pascal's "Kneel down and you will believe!" has to be understood as involving a kind of self-referential causality: "Kneel down and you will believe that you knelt down because you believed!" The second thing is that, in the "normal" cynical functioning of ideology, belief is displaced onto another, onto a "subject supposed to believe," so that the true logic is: "Kneel down and you will thereby MAKE SOMEONE ELSE BELIEVE!" … To believe "directly," without the externalizing mediation of a ritual – is a heavy, oppressing, traumatic burden, which, through exerting a ritual, one has a chance of transferring onto an Other … Let us take the affirmation "I believe." Its negation is: "I do not really believe, I just fake to believe." However, its properly Hegelian negation of negation is not the return to direct belief, but the self-relating fake: "I fake to fake to believe," which means: "I really believe without being aware of it." Is, then, irony not the ultimate form of the critique of ideology today – irony in the precise Mozartean sense of taking the statements more seriously than the subjects who utter them themselves?' Žižek, 'What's Wrong with Fundamentalism?', www.lacan.com/zizpassion.htm (accessed 30 November 2015).

15　For a thorough study of this successful antiracist campaign, see Dave Rich, *Zionists and Anti-Zionists: Political Protest and Student Activism in Britain, 1968–1986*, PhD thesis (Birkbeck College, University of London, 2015).

16　On the escalation of antisemitic violence in France in recent years, see the five part series in *Tablet* by Marc Weitzmann, www.tabletmag.com/tag/frances-toxic-hate and also Marie Brenner, 'France's Scarlet Letter', www.vanityfair.com/news/2003/06/france-muslim-jewish-population (both accessed 20 October 2015).

17　Timothy Garton Ash, 'Defying the Assassin's Veto', *New York Review of Books*, 19 February 2015, www.nybooks.com/articles/2015/02/19/defying-assassins-veto/.

18　Richard Seymour in the *Jacobin* described the demonstration as 'platitudinous, mawkish and narcissistic' – a 'blackmail that forces us into solidarity with a racist institution'. It became something of a vogue to say 'Je ne suis pas Charlie'. Jon Wilson in *Labour List* referred to what he called the 'obvious racism' of *Charlie Hebdo*. Jacob Garfield in the *Hooded Utilitarian* described *Charlie Hebdo* as 'xenophobic, racist, sexist, homophobic, and anti-Islamic' and claimed its editorial board was all-white, as if this were itself a damning argument. It was actually quite untrue – one of the murdered journalists was the Algerian, Moustapha Ourrad.

19　Mehdi Hasan 'As a Muslim, I'm Fed Up With the Hypocrisy of the Free Speech Fundamentalists', *New Statesman*, 13 January, 2015, www.newstatesman.com/mehdi-hasan/2015/01/muslim-i-m-fed-hypocrisy-free-speech-fundamentalists (accessed 10 May 2015).

20 For a probing analysis of the Satanic Verses controversy see Kenan Malik, *From Fatwa to Jihad: The Rushdie Affair and its Legacy* (London: Atlantic Books, 2009).

21 In 1979 the Monty Python film *Life of Brian* was treated as blasphemous by various religious groups and local authorities in the UK and the US. It was condemned as such by Malcolm Muggeridge and Mervyn Stockwood, the Bishop of Southwark, in a BBC televised debate.

22 See Paul Berman's compelling reflections on this aspect of the Charlie Hebdo affair in *Tablet* (14 January 2015 and 26 May 2015) 'The Charlie Cover', www.tabletmag.com/jewish-arts-and-culture/books/188320/the-charlie-cover; and 'Cruelty & Perversity: Postprandial Reflections on the PEN Protesters. The Grim Satire of the "Charlie Hebdo" Controversy, in Context', www.tabletmag.com/jewish-arts-and-culture/books/191181/reflections-on-pen-protesters (both accessed 12 June 2015). One issue concerns the economy of compassion that responds with justified compassion to the sufferings of Palestinians only to convert compassion for the victim into hatred of the victimiser or those it holds guilty of causing the suffering of Palestinians. It neglects other sources of victimisation of Palestinians and the interests ordinary Palestinians have in opposing antisemitism, not least when it is deployed by their own political leaders as a means of internal repression.

23 Kenan Malik writes: 'The impact of censorship is in fact to undermine progressive movements within minority communities. Take the controversy over the Danish cartoons. There's a general assumption that all Muslims were offended by the cartoons and that all Muslims wished to ban them. Not true … The multiculturalist censor demands respect not just for the person but also for his or her beliefs. And in so doing they undermine individual autonomy, both by constraining the right of people to criticise others' beliefs and by insisting that individuals who hold those beliefs are too weak or vulnerable to stand up to criticism, satire or abuse'. Intelligence Debate, Royal Geographical Society, London 7 June 2006, www.kenanmalik.com/debates/free_speech_IQ2.html (accessed 30 November 2015).

24 Some Iranian and Arab media claimed that Israel, through its secret service, Mossad, orchestrated the attacks and planned the attacks in order to punish France for recognising Palestine as a state or to discredit Muslims. See Marc Weitzmann, 'The Failure of Intelligent Explanations: France Grapples with the Aftermath of Attacks that are no Longer "Just Against Jews"', *Tablet*, 25 November 2015, www.tabletmag.com/jewish-news-and-politics/195371/france-intelligent-explanations (accessed 20 October 2016).

25 The attack on the Bataclan music venue may not have been chosen at random. It had already figured for some time as a potential target of antizionist violence perhaps because it had, until recently before the massacres, Jewish owners, www.lepoint.fr/societe/le-bataclan-une-cible-regulierement-visee-14-11-2015-1981544_23.php (accessed 25 July 2016).

26 Hannah Arendt drew the concepts of 'common sense' and 'enlarged mentality' from her reading of Kant's *Critique of Judgment*. See Hannah Arendt, *Lectures on Kant's Political Philosophy* (Chicago: University of Chicago Press, 1982).

27 For powerful critical analyses of contemporary left antisemitism from the left, see David Hirsh 'The Corbyn Left: Politics of Position and Politics of Reason', *Fathom*,

Autumn 2015, http://fathomjournal.org/the-corbyn-left-the-politics-of-position-and-the-politics-of-reason/ (accessed 30 November 2015); Alan Johnson, 'The Left and the Jews: Time for a Rethink', *Fathom*, Autumn 2015, http://fathomjournal.org/the-left-and-the-jews-time-for-a-rethink/ (accessed 30 November 2015); Michael Walzer, 'Islamism and the Left', *Dissent*, Winter 2015 www.dissentmagazine.org/article/islamism-and-the-left (accessed 30 November 2015).

28 Some see Israel as the instrument of Western neo-imperialism in the Middle East and some go further in viewing Israel as controlling policy-making in the US and Britain. This reversion was first presented to an academic audience in John Mearsheimer and Stephen M. Walt, *The Israel lobby and U.S. Foreign Policy* (New York: Farrar, Straus and Giroux, 2007).

29 We may point to failures within much of the European left to show solidarity with the Iraqi opposition under Saddam or with the Iranian 'Green Revolution' of 2009–2010, and conversely the enthusiasm within some sections of the European left for Hezbollah, Hamas and jihadi movements opposed to the West. Dualist thinking today mirrors uncritical support in the past for the regimes of Nasser in Egypt or the Ba'ath in Syria in spite of the fact that these regimes oppressed and killed their own domestic left-wing oppositions. For a moving analysis of neglected human rights struggles against Islamic fundamentalism, see Karima Bennoune, *Your Fatwa Does Not Apply Here: Untold Stories from the Fight Against Muslim Fundamentalism* (New York: W.W. Norton and Co, 2013).

30 For an insightful discussion of reflexivity and positionality see Glynis Cousin, 'Positioning Positionality: The Reflexive Turn' in Maggie Savin-Baden and Claire Howell Major (eds.), *New Approaches to Qualitative Research: Wisdom and Uncertainty* (London: Routledge Education, 2010), 9–18.

Index